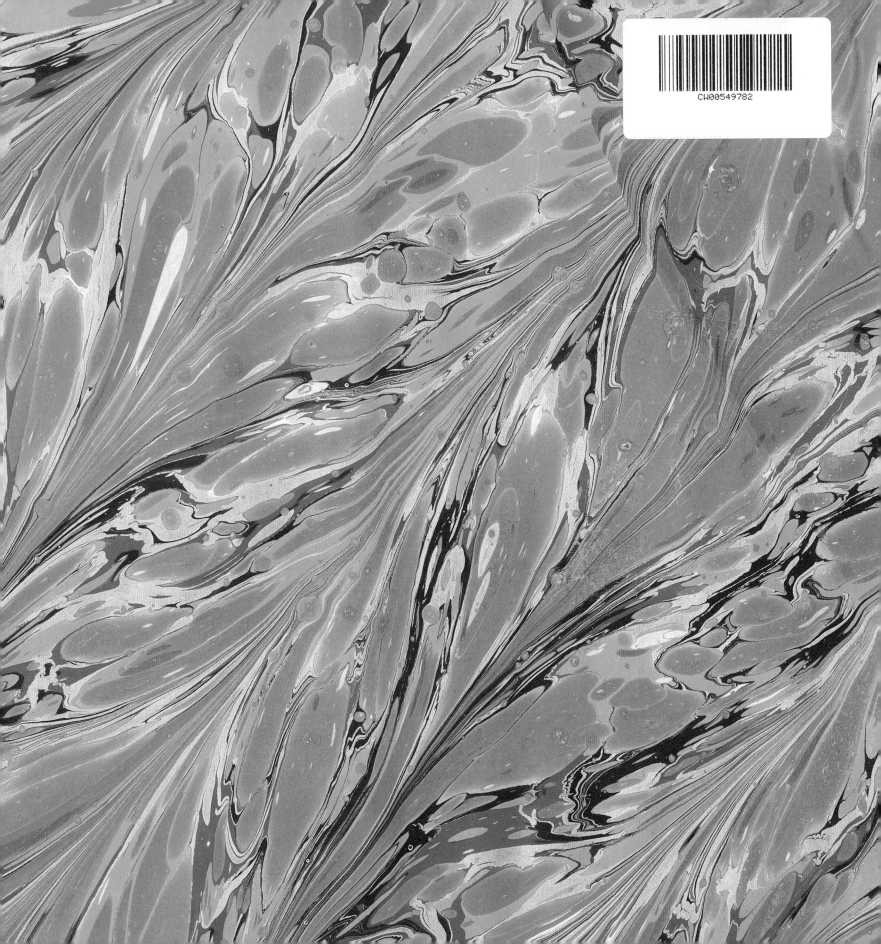

CONTEMPORARY
PAPER MARBLING

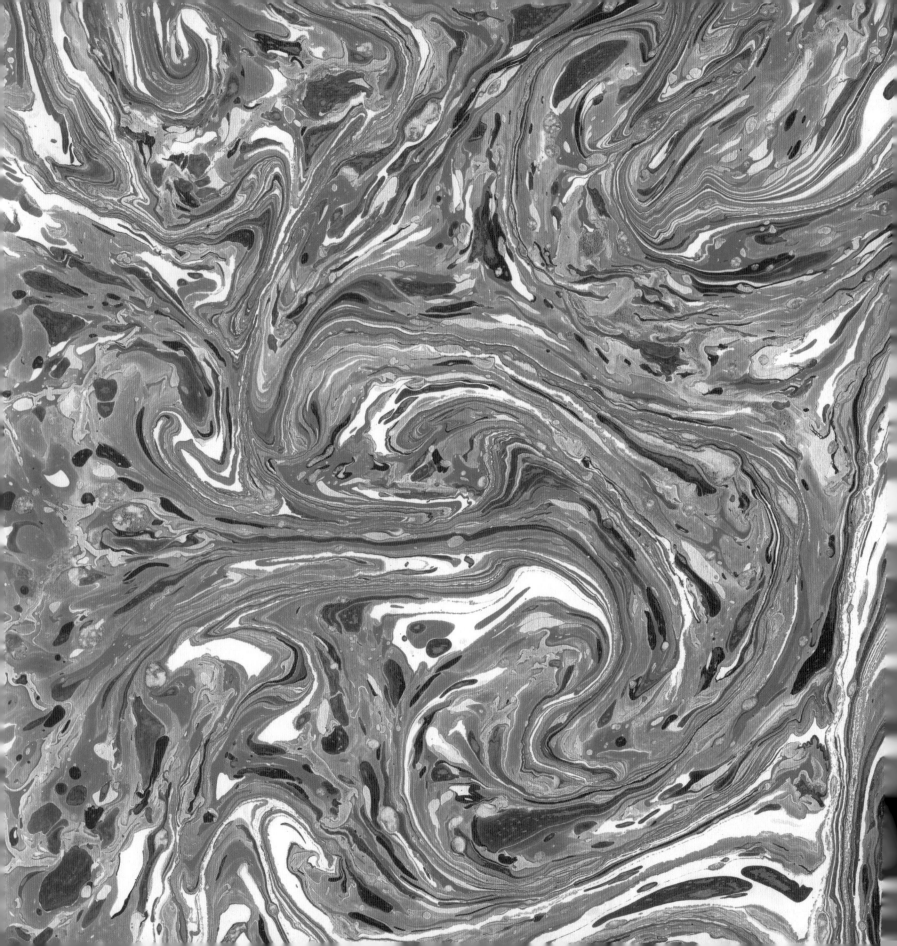

CONTEMPORARY
PAPER MARBLING

Lucy McGrath

BATSFORD

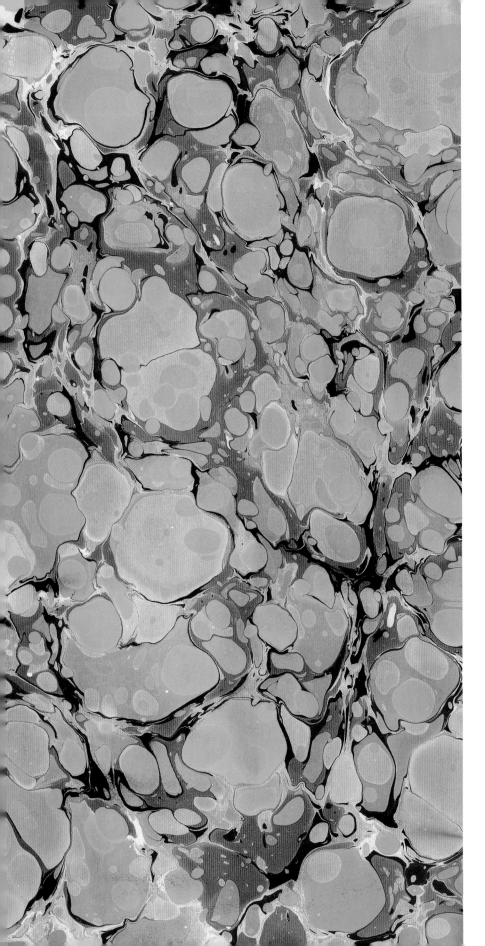

For Mum and Dad

First published in the United Kingdom in 2019 by
Batsford
43 Great Ormond Street
London WC1N 3HZ
An imprint of Pavilion Books Company Ltd

ISBN: 9781849945530

A CIP catalogue record for this book is available from the
British Library.

10 9 8 7 6 5 4 3 2 1
25 24 23 22 21 20 19

Reproduction by Rival Colour Ltd, UK
Printed and bound by Toppan Leefung Printing Ltd, China

This book can be ordered direct from the publisher at
www.pavilionbooks.com or try your local bookshop.

Distributed in the United States and Canada by
Sterling Publishing Co., Inc.,
1166 Avenue of the Americas, 17th Floor, New York, NY 10036

Contents

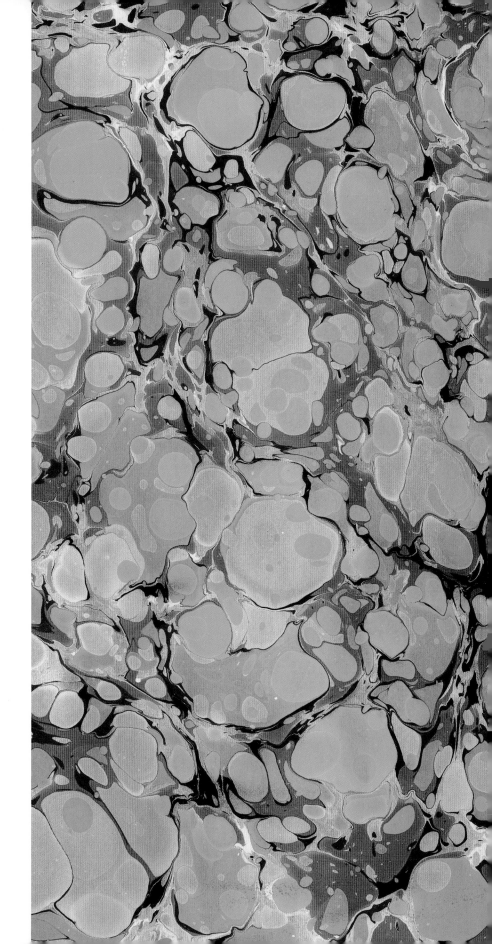

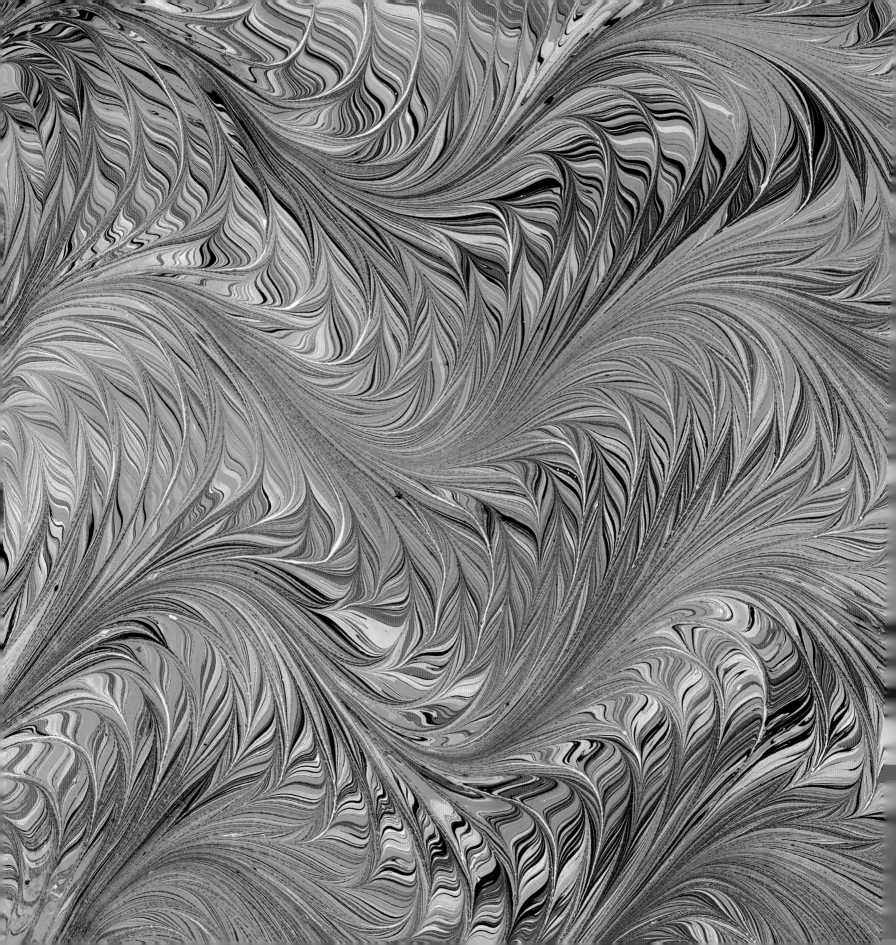

INTRODUCTION

My story

I've always loved books, particularly old, unassuming books with dog-eared covers that hide beautiful works of marbled art on their endpapers.

Books are very much linked to the art of marbling; they're the vehicle that propelled marbling to its heyday in the Victorian era. I learnt how to bind books at university, and that was when I decided to try my hand at marbling. It was a complete disaster. It wasn't until a holiday in Turkey, five years later, that I tried again, led by a local marbler at the hotel where I was staying. This time it worked – and I was completely enchanted by the chaos and beauty of it.

Back in the UK, I sought out a course with English marbler Victoria Hall, which was a very different experience from Turkish marbling and inspired me even further. I carried on experimenting and trying out techniques, colours and materials, developing my own style. Sadly, marbling is an endangered craft in the UK, so I am on a mission to modernize it: to help carve a new niche for it, perhaps separate from books, and pass on the techniques so others can enjoy its peculiar delights well into the future.

Since starting my marbling brand, Marmor Paperie, I've worked with companies such as Matches Fashion and Molton Brown, and my work has featured in publications including *Country Life*, *Homes & Gardens* and *Stylist*.

PREVIOUS PAGE Cockerell
Wave pattern (see page 108).

RIGHT Swirl pattern in fresh
pastel tones.

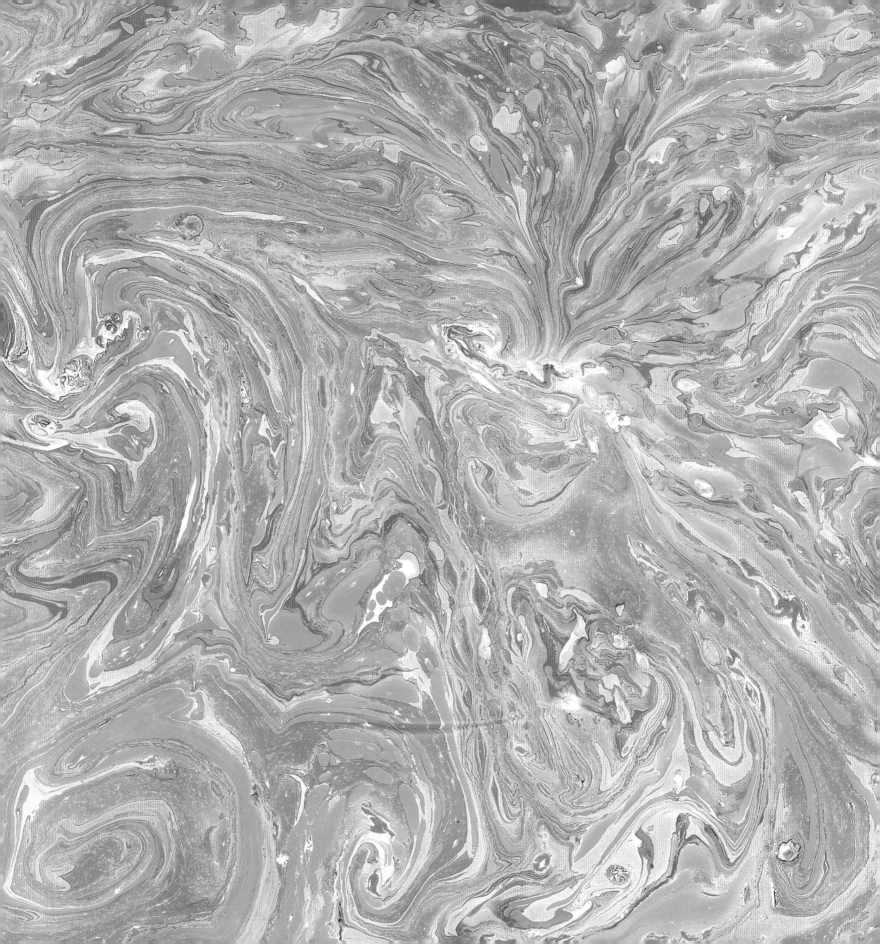

History

Marbling is a unique craft, sitting somewhere between painting, printmaking and science.

The first known form of marbling comes from Japan: a delicate, meditative technique called *suminagashi*. The earliest known examples date as far back as the twelfth century, but the technique may have been practised even earlier.

Suminagashi was different from the style of marbling we practise today due to its omission of a thickening agent in the marbling liquid – it simply used sumi ink on plain water. The eddies and currents present in the unthickened water are a design feature, marked with bands of black and white.

It is thought that *suminagashi* and some knowledge of its technique travelled down the Silk Road trading routes, arriving in Turkey where a new method of 'painting on water' was developed around the thirteenth or fourteenth century. This Turkish tradition saw the introduction of a thickened size, and more colourful pieces of work. It was used to decorate the borders of calligraphy artwork and fine bindings of religious texts.

Trade routes again brought the art into Europe, probably through the cosmopolitan port of Venice, and it spread quickly into Germany and France where intricate combed patterns were developed. Paper marblers were extremely secretive about their techniques, guarding their art carefully to prevent competition. It wasn't until 1853 that a detailed description of marbling and its techniques was published by Charles Woolnough in *The Whole Art of Marbling*, when marbling started to become more widely practised.

The techniques used in marbling have barely changed over the centuries – the engraving opposite shows a bustling eighteenth-century marbling studio – if you look closely, you can see from the far right forcing the size through a sieve, hanging papers to dry on lines, pulling a rake through the marbling bath, dropping paint from brushes onto the bath; laying the paper down onto the surface to pick up the paint and on the far left, grinding the pigments used to make paint.

Some of these steps have been modernized or improved, but this process and these tools are essentially the same as those you will soon be using.

ABOVE Engraving from
Recueil de Planches, published
in 1767, showing workers in
a marbling workshop.

Marbling now

Marbling in Europe has been very closely tied to the bookbinding and printing industries – marbled endpapers became common in the Victorian era and, as printing boomed, marbling also enjoyed its heyday.

As publishers vied to find cheaper and more efficient ways of producing books, demand for marbled endpapers and covers declined – making marbled papers takes a certain amount of time and skill, which meant they were a more expensive option than mass-produced papers printed using machines. By the end of the nineteenth century, marbling had fallen out of favour.

The final nail in the coffin came with the introduction of digital scanning and printing in the 1990s – now photographic reproductions of marbled papers can simply be printed without the need to touch any paint at all! And photo-editing software allows many different colourways to be generated from just one paper. There is no demand for marbling as an industrial skill any more – which means there are very few professional paper marblers left in the business.

LEFT Paper lanterns can be marbled by rolling them through a large bath of size.

RIGHT This marbled concrete plant pot is an example of the many different surfaces that can be marbled.

The future of marbling

Technology has advanced very quickly in the last century, and lots of traditional craftspeople have found their skills surplus to requirements.

I think this heralds a new and exciting era for marbling – it is no longer restricted by the needs of the publishing industry and can now blossom into something all its own, something exciting and beautiful.

In a world increasingly full of mass-manufacturing and cookie-cutter products, marbling can take on a new importance as an art form in its own right: its chaotic technique, organic look and the fact that each piece is unique set it apart. I want to take inspiration from the marbling of the past, but experiment with it and push it in new directions – trying out new techniques, new paints and new materials to change the way people think about marbling.

RIGHT A circular ceramic tile provides the perfect canvas for this hypnotic swirled art piece.

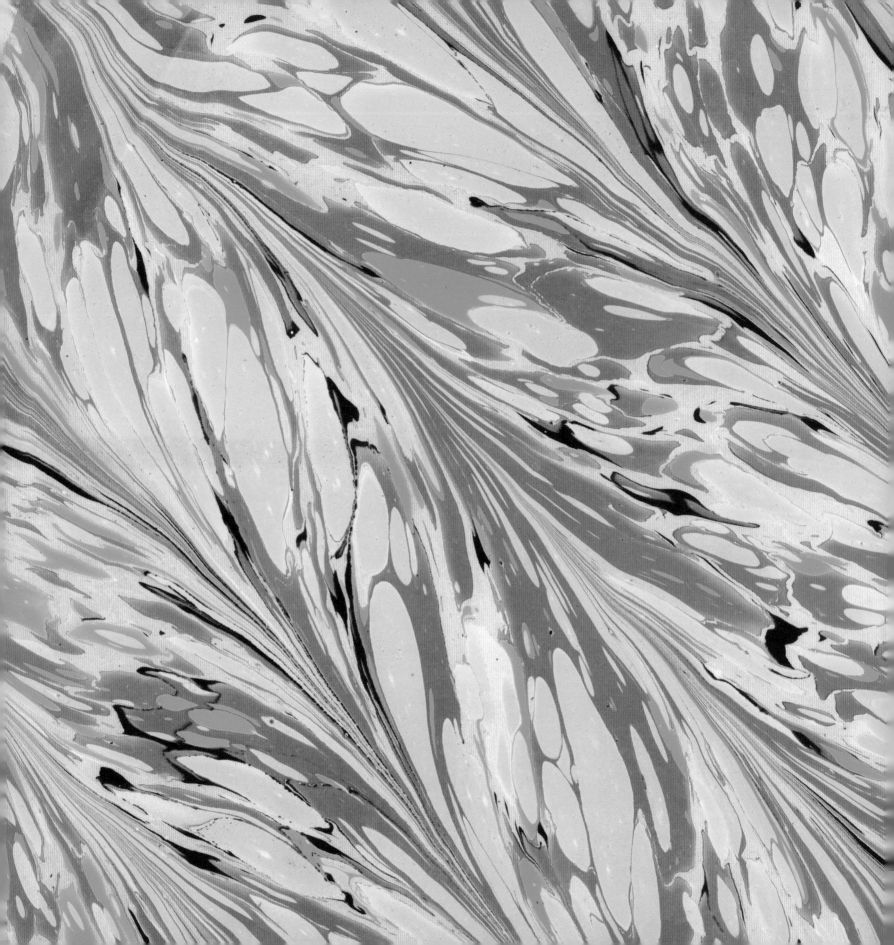

PREPARATION

Equipment

Marbling does not require lots of expensive specialist equipment – in fact most of what you'll need can be found at home.

- Shallow tray or container to hold liquid (larger than the dimensions of your paper)
- Range of paint brushes
- Bamboo skewers or similar
- Washing-up liquid
- Pipettes
- Eyedroppers
- Jars (200ml or so)
- Airer or washing line and pegs
- Jug
- Board to rinse paper on
- Rake(s)
- Newspaper
- Blender
- Measuring spoons
- Digital scales
- Sponge
- Small heat-proof container
- Pencil

Materials

- Carrageenan powder (see page 20)
- Paint (see page 26)
- Paper (see page 29)
- Alum (see page 30)

PREVIOUS PAGE Feather pattern (see page 82).

LEFT All the materials and equipment you need to begin marbling are easy to source.

Making the size

Marbling owes its magic to one vital but unassuming ingredient: seaweed. Mixed with water, it forms a gloopy, viscous liquid referred to as 'size'. This is poured into your tray and is ultimately what causes the paint to float and hold its characteristic fluid shapes.

So what exactly is it?

The key ingredient is a kind of seaweed called carrageen, also known as 'Irish moss', and commonly found on the rocky shores of Ireland (and along the Atlantic coastline). It contains a thickening agent called carrageenan which is extracted and turned into a powder that can be easily blended with water to the right consistency. Until just a few decades ago, marblers had to boil the seaweed in a vat for hours, strain it through cheesecloth and let it cool before use – a strenuous task!

Carrageenan comes in three different variations: iota, kappa and lambda. Look for the lambda type, as the others are more commonly used for creating gels and substances more on the solid end of the spectrum.

How does it work?

Carrageenan is a natural thickening agent, much like agar or gelatin. It forms a viscous liquid (not quite a gel – about the consistency of wallpaper paste) when mixed with water, allowing for a much higher surface tension than water would normally have. This surface tension causes paint dropped onto it to float rather than assimilate into the mixture. Its density also means it holds its shape when manipulated, so the paint on the surface can be controlled much more easily.

RIGHT Carrageen seaweed
in its natural form and
carrageenan powder.

WHAT YOU NEED FOR A BEGINNER'S BATH (FITS A4 PAPER)

- Digital scales
- 13g (¹/₂oz) of powdered carrageenan
- Blender (carrageenan is totally natural and non-toxic so don't be afraid to use what's already in your kitchen)
- 2 litres (3¹/₂ pints) of water – you can use tap water, but metal deposits or bacteria in your pipes may affect the size, so filtered or distilled water is a safer bet
- Shallow container, a little larger than A4 paper dimensions

METHOD

1 Place the carrageenan into the blender and add around 400ml (14fl oz) of the water. Blitz for 30 seconds or until there are no visible clumps of powder.

2 Pour in the remaining water and blend for 30 seconds or until the mixture is homogeneous. It will be full of tiny bubbles but shouldn't have lumps or visible 'bits'.

3 Decant the size into your tray and let it sit for at least 6 hours (overnight is best) while the mixture settles and the bubbles pop.

How to store your size

In hotter surroundings (above 25°C / 77°F) it is better to store your size in a refrigerator overnight to reduce the risk of bacteria growth. Be sure to give it time to warm up, though, as the temperature of the size affects the spread of paint.

Cover your size whenever you aren't using it to prevent dust and bacteria from getting in. It should be good for 2–3 days of marbling depending on temperature and how heavily it's used – paint can sink into the size and muddy it, making it hard to see what you're doing. It's often easier to start afresh when this happens.

Are there alternatives to carrageenan?

If you're struggling to find carrageenan, there are a few other options for thickening water, but none hold fine detail quite as well (in my opinion!). Methyl cellulose mixed with water is a popular choice in Turkey and warmer climates – it keeps much longer than carrageenan, too. There's also a substance called gum tragacanth, which is made from the sap of plants found in the Middle East. This is the traditional ingredient for size, used for centuries until carrageenan gradually replaced it.

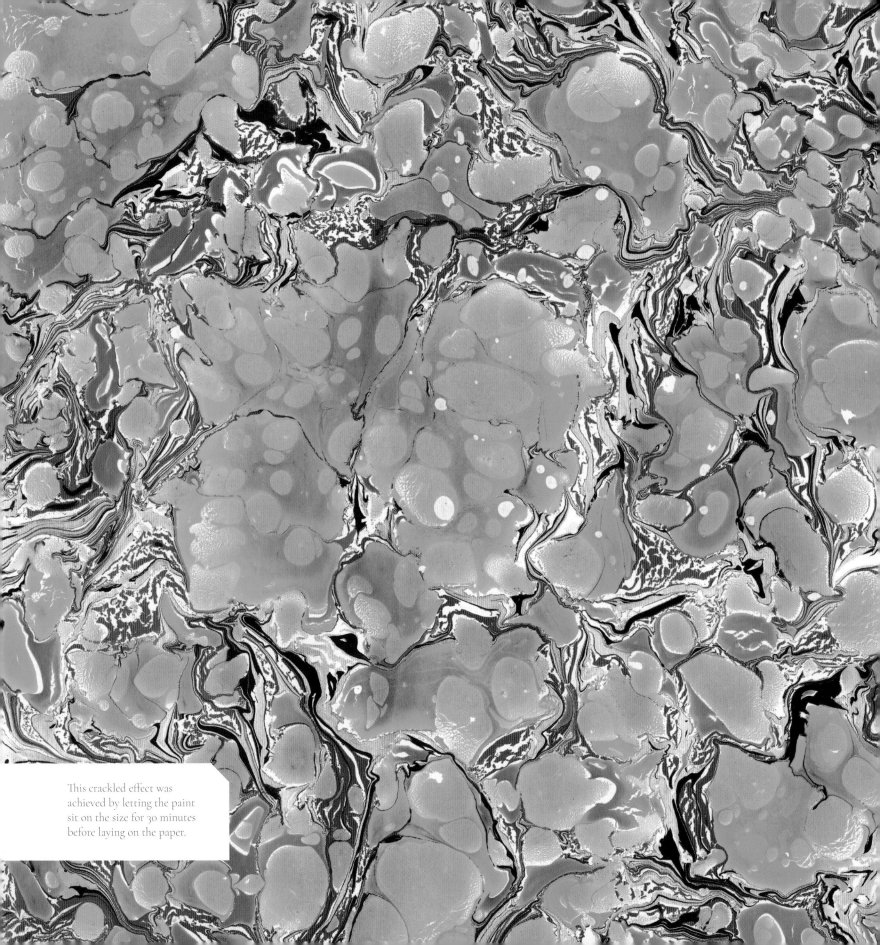

This crackled effect was achieved by letting the paint sit on the size for 30 minutes before laying on the paper.

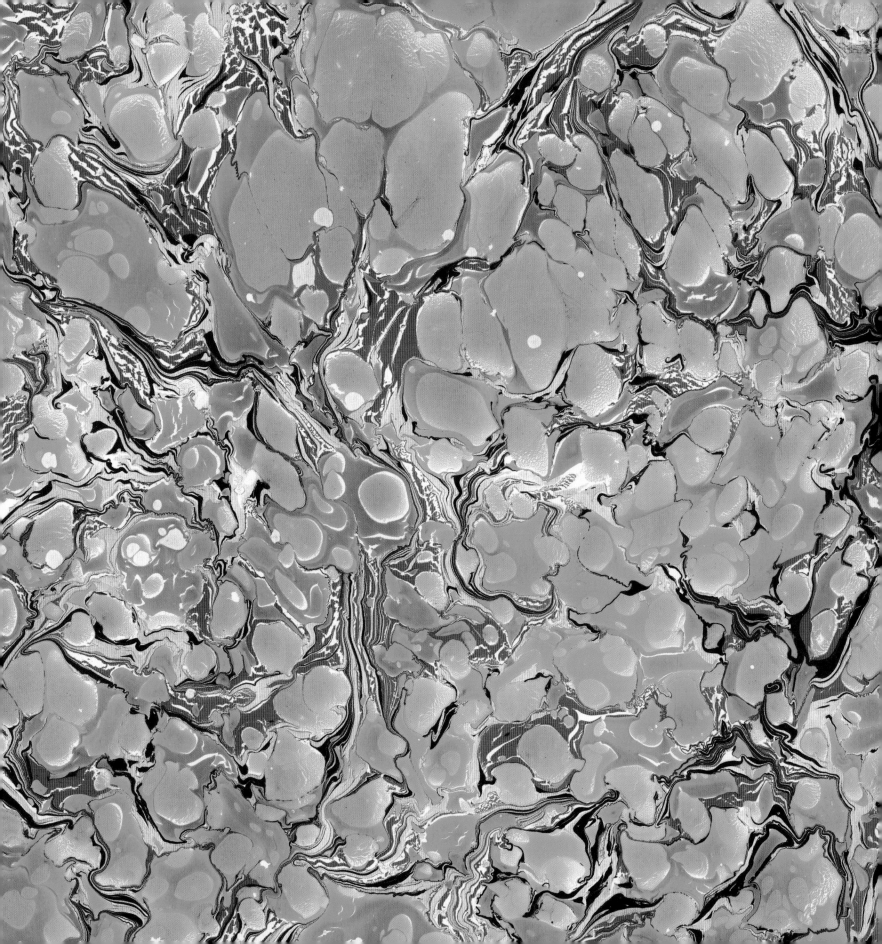

Paint to use

Once of the great things about marbling is that there's no single right way to do it, so there are lots of options available to you. The type of paint you use is up to you.

Watercolour or gouache

Traditionally, marblers used watercolours or gouache on a thickened-water size. These remain the easiest paints to control so may be a good place to start. You will need to add a wetting agent – a solution called 'ox gall' – to the paints to increase how much they disperse over the size (see page 44). Ox gall is an animal product so, for a vegan alternative, heavily diluted dish soap can work – or use acrylic paints instead. Watercolours and gouache are easy to obtain at most art stores and work together well, though they can be less durable and less vivid than acrylics.

Acrylic paint

Acrylics are my preferred medium – though they can be difficult to control and require a lot of testing and tweaking. But they allow you to marble onto a range of materials – including fabric – and, since the binder that carries the pigments is essentially plastic, have a lot of strength so are less likely to rub away or degrade. See page 46 for more information on using acrylics.

Oil paints

These are naturally hydrophobic (water repellent) paints that will float on the surface of plain water – so you do not need to use a thickened-water size. This makes them a great option for dipping your toes into the marbling technique! This does have limitations, though – plain water won't hold any shapes, so it's impossible to make controlled patterns. The paint will also bead up on the surface of the water rather than spreading out in smooth swathes. See page 96 for instructions on using oil paints.

RIGHT A selection of paints and brushes, and a palette for mixing colours.

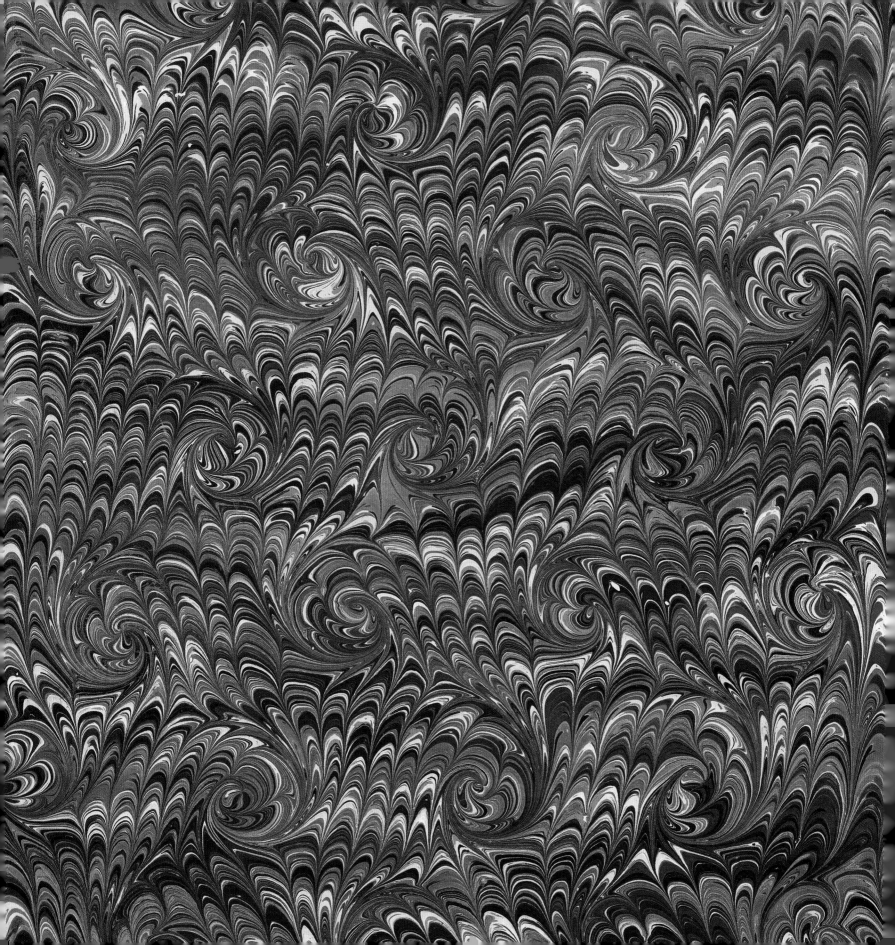

Choosing paper

Marbling is very versatile and works really well on all kinds of papers, from plain old printer paper through to luxury laid card.

There are a few things to bear in mind when choosing paper:

- The thinner the paper, the more likely it is to disintegrate when wet – I don't recommend anything less than 80gsm.
- If the paper is too thick, you risk losing flexibility and ending up with air bubbles in your pattern. Anything thicker than 300gsm may prove tricky.
- Avoid paper that is described as 'sized' and especially glossy papers – the paint will not be able to adhere to the shiny surface very well.
- Equally, avoid papers that are highly absorbent such as watercolour paper as the paint will sink into the uneven surface and lose its vibrancy.

LEFT a traditional French Curl pattern using bold, modern colours (see page 104).

Have fun with your paper choices; you can get great results marbling onto coloured paper, patterned paper (particularly geometrics) and handmade paper.

Preparing paper with a mordant

Before any paint touches your paper, you must make sure you prepare your paper with a mordant. Mordants are substances that fix pigment to a surface, commonly used in processes like textile dyeing and leather tanning. Forgetting to mordant your paper will stop the paint from adhering to it – and there is nothing more heartbreaking than watching your beautiful marbling wash away before your eyes as you rinse it.

Aluminium potassium sulphate, also known as 'alum', is the mordant that works best for marbling. It is widely available at a low cost, and comes in powdered, granular and crystal forms. I recommend granules as they dissolve more quickly than crystal shards and are less likely to make a mess than powder.

Safety information

Be careful when using alum, as it can be dangerous at high concentrations. Make sure you are working in a well-ventilated room and try to avoid breathing in steam when dissolving it. Wear gloves when handling it, as it can irritate the skin.

WHAT YOU NEED FOR 25 A4 SHEETS

- Digital scales
- 8g (¹/₄oz) aluminium potassium sulphate (alum)
- Glass jar or heatproof bowl
- 100ml (3¹/₂ fl oz) freshly boiled water
- Small heatproof container
- Pencil
- A4 paper (up to 25 sheets)
- Sponge

METHOD

1 Measure your alum into a glass jar or heatproof bowl and pour in the freshly boiled water. Stir to dissolve.

2 When the alum has fully dissolved, pour the solution into a small heatproof container.

3 Take a pencil and mark the back of your papers with an X. This is how you will know which side has not been mordanted when marbling.

4 Put your first paper X-side down on your table.

5 Using a sponge, take some of the solution and spread it across your paper as evenly as possible. Be careful not to oversaturate your paper, but also ensure you put enough on to cover the surface fully.

6 Put the sheet aside, wet side facing up, and lay out the next sheet as in step 4.

7 Repeat step 5 but, when finished, lay your sheet on top of the previous sheet, wet side to wet side, X facing up. Smooth to get rid of air bubbles or creases. This ensures your papers will dry flat.

8 Repeat steps 5–7, stacking papers dry side to dry side, wet to wet.

9 Cover your stack of paper with something heavy to keep it flat while drying.

It's best to use your paper when it's still slightly damp – around 10–15 minutes after mordanting should be enough. This means your paper will be more flexible when you place it on the marbling bath – much easier than trying to wrestle with warped or buckled dry sheets.

If you find your papers are too dry, you can use a spray bottle to mist them with alum solution. Make sure there's no liquid on the surface of the paper when you marble it, though.

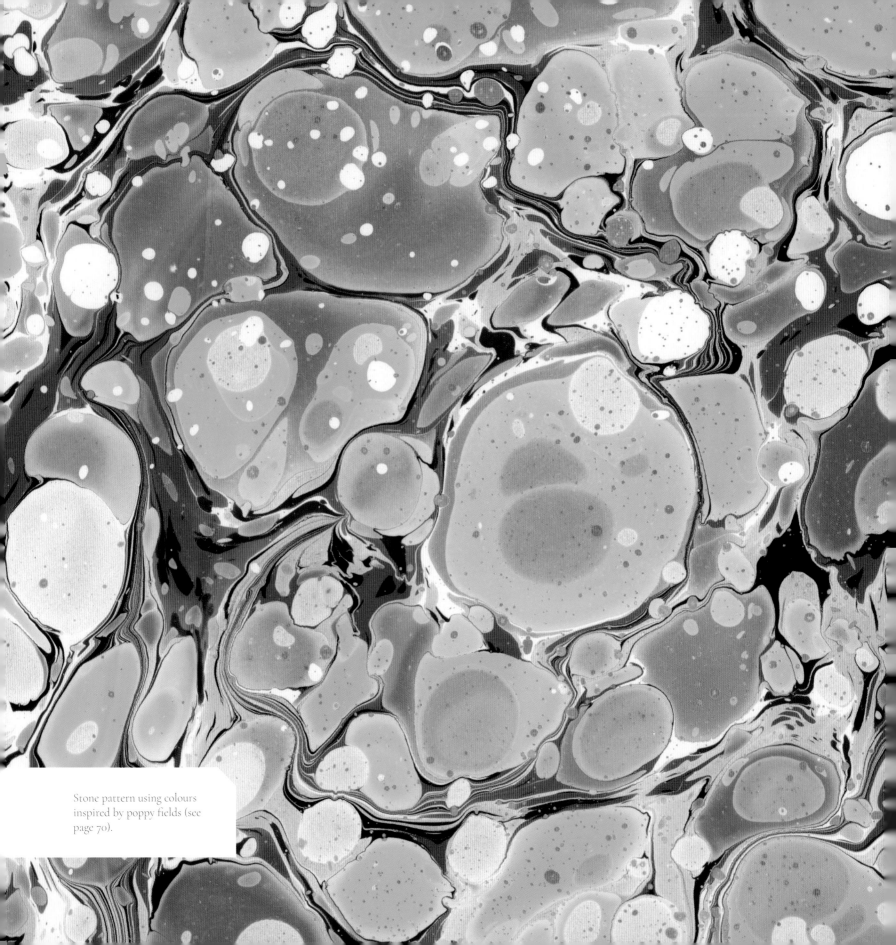

Stone pattern using colours inspired by poppy fields (see page 70).

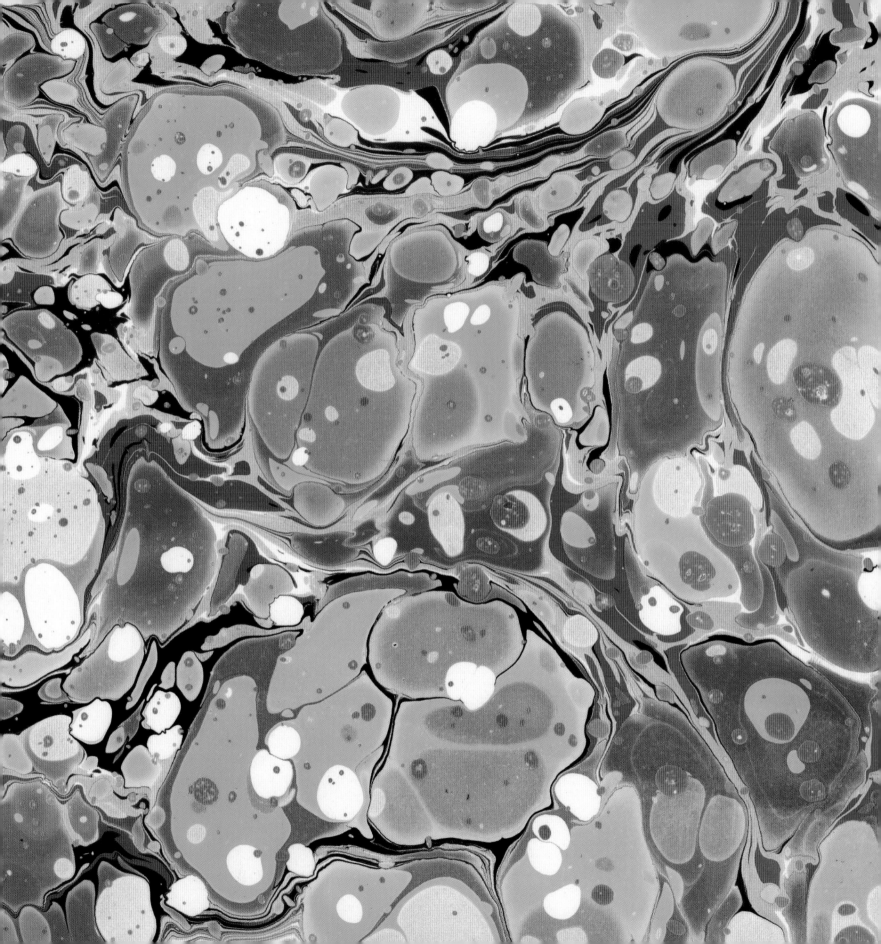

Planning your design

Looking for inspiration

It can be hard to know where to start when you're trying marbling for the first time. You might have seen many intricate or impressive designs that you'd like to try – but I recommend putting those out of your mind, at least for your first few sessions, and letting your ideas grow organically as you get comfortable and play with the paints and their effects.

Once your size is prepared, your papers are mordanted and your tools are ready, it is time to start getting creative. The colours you choose are the most important part of marbling – how they behave together; their brightness and saturation; how much they disperse on the size – these are what give marbled paper its character.

RIGHT An inspiration board based on autumnal moods and colours.

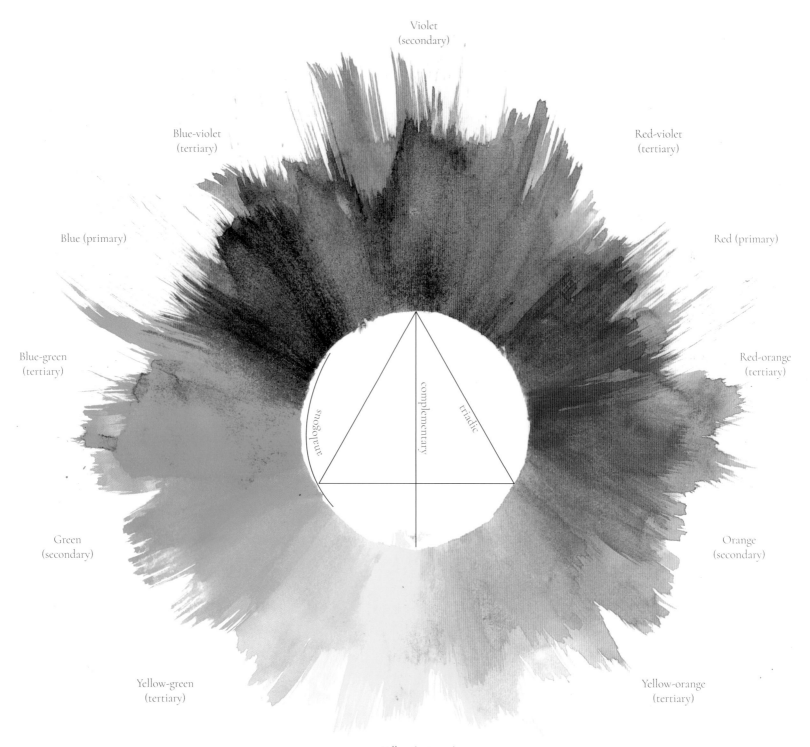

Violet
(secondary)

Blue-violet
(tertiary)

Red-violet
(tertiary)

Blue (primary)

Red (primary)

Blue-green
(tertiary)

Red-orange
(tertiary)

analogous

complementary

triadic

Green
(secondary)

Orange
(secondary)

Yellow-green
(tertiary)

Yellow-orange
(tertiary)

Yellow (primary)

Colour theory

A basic knowledge of colour theory will help when choosing which colours you want to work with.

The colours on the wheel can be split into three types:

- **Primary** – yellow, red and blue; these cannot be formed by mixing other colours. You need these colours to make all other hues.
- **Secondary** – orange, violet and green; these can be made by mixing two primary colours.
- **Tertiary** – these are formed when a primary colour is mixed with a secondary colour.

You can use the wheel as a guide to help choose colours that will work well together.

- **Analogous colours:** any three colours that sit next to each other on the wheel will work harmoniously together in a palette.
- **Complementary colours:** any two colours that are exactly opposite each other on the wheel are known as 'complementary' – these contrast sharply so are great for adding interest or 'pop'.
- **Triadic colours:** three colours that are equidistant from each other on the wheel will form a triadic colour scheme. You see this a lot in traditional marbling, where combinations of oxblood red, deep blue and ochre are quite common.

Tips on picking your colours for marbling:

- I often choose three analogous colours with one being slightly dominant, then add a complementary to make both colours 'pop' and add visual interest.
- Think about using black in your colour schemes – black, grey and darker tones of your main colours help to ground the scheme, adding contrast that in turn makes the brighter colours appear richer.
- Metallic colours such as gold, copper and silver are exciting to use – but don't forget they have a place on the colour wheel too, one that may or may not work well with other colours you are using.
- A light sprinkle of a complementary colour can be a good way to finish a design.

We have only scratched the surface of the huge topic that is colour theory – it is definitely worth exploring this area in more detail. Simply experimenting with colours to see for yourself what works and what doesn't also goes a long way to help!

LEFT Colour wheel showing the primary, secondary and tertiary colours, with the complementary, analogous and triadic schemes.

Inspiration boards

I'm always looking around me for inspiration – it can come from the most unlikely places. Perhaps a deep green moss on a discoloured brick wall, a rose-tinted sunset, a bowl full of juicy nectarines, even an advertisement hoarding.

An inspiration or mood board can be an effective way to develop and clarify your ideas of what you want to evoke with your marbled paper. It's best to use one piece as a starting point and build around that – it could be a beautiful image from a magazine, a photo you've taken of something that appealed to you, an object you like or a piece of fabric.

Put that in the centre of your board and start building up items that complement it. Try to use lots of different kinds of things that help to add depth to your idea. You might want to consider looking for items in each of these categories:

- **Texture** – different types of paper; knitted or woven fabric; a piece of cotton; wood; a tree trunk; leaves.
- **Colours** – swatches of colour that might be drawn from your initial item. You can paint these yourself or use cut-outs from magazines, swatch books or coloured paper. Play around with lots of different combinations until you find ones that you like.
- **Mood** – find images that complement your original item; for instance, for a photo of a sunflower, you could find images of French fields, photos of rooms decorated in deep yellow, a Mediterranean farmhouse, and so on.
- **Objects** – consider using pressed flowers, found objects, shards of seaglass, bottlecaps or ephemera such as bits of packaging and handwritten notes.

Digital mood boards

I've found a wealth of inspiration from the internet – and there are amazing websites and apps that help you navigate the vast seas of online content by building digital mood boards, such as Pinterest, GoMoodboard or InVision. By keeping it digital, you can add as many images as you want, editing and changing their positions as you go, and you can avoid having to print pictures out, saving on ink and paper.

However, everyone has their own ways of working – some prefer the immediacy of physical boards and collections of items, while others like the range and convenience that digital boards allow. You may not even be a visual mood board kind of person – there is no right or wrong with inspiration; go with whatever works best for you!

RIGHT Inspiration boards collect and capture ideas from all around you and help to translate texture, colour and mood into your work.

'Double-marbled' paper that has been marbled a second time once the first layer has dried (see page 111).

Finalizing your palette

Once you have built up your inspiration board, you'll find that you have a clear idea of the kind of mood you want to evoke and the colours that will help you to do that. Perhaps certain colours make an appearance again and again? It's time to start making swatches and finalizing your palette!

It's best to start with at least four colours but no more than six. You can add more as you become more experienced and build up more complex colour palettes. Pick a colour that stood out from your mood board and work up a palette – look back to the section on colour theory for some tips on how to choose a harmonious colour scheme. Mix the chosen colours with your preferred paints. On a piece of paper, draw out a line of 4–6 squares. Make a few more similar rows of squares below.

Paint each of the squares with one of your mixed colours and reflect on your palette – does a certain shade dominate? Is it too dark or too light? Warm or cold? Could a complementary colour help to add interest?

If you're happy with your colours, go ahead and move on to the next step – testing them on the size. You may find that you want to make some adjustments, or try a different combination, in which case paint the next line of squares using adjusted colours. Carry on like this until you are really happy with your palette.

RIGHT It's a good idea to note the paint mixes you use on a piece of paper so you can try to match them if you want to re-create the colours in the future.

Tip

Many people shy away from using black or grey in favour of brighter, more exciting colours. However, I recommend using black as it is a great way to ground your palette, bringing an element of contrast that helps the other colours to sing.

② - S...

1st att...

Eau...

① - Coral & ...p Blue + Gold/Copper?

1st att...

Blue ... quoise deep - Liquix HB

 1 = quinacridone red, liqui HB
 + Sys3 white - 40%   20%
 + Sys3 yellow - 20%
 + cad. red - liqui H B - 20%

— WAY TOO DISPERSEY

Coral 2 = cad red - liqui HB - 55
 + sys 3 yellow 20
 + sys 3 white 20
 + grey (tiny lil bit of mixed black + white)   (liqui s13) 5

2nd ...

Liqui...

(cad red
white

glass + (G)
pro mag (6ah)

pro mag (
ultramarine (G)
tubile

(more
at 3)

North red (G)
white +
+ yellow (+ bg)
+ black (snow)

①   80

Testing paint on the size

Mixing the colours you want is an important step, but their behaviour on the size can completely change their tone and character. Marbling is based on colours floating and spreading out across the surface of the size, and the colours become lighter the more they spread out.

It is a good idea to put a small batch of size in a baking tray or A5-size container before you start, so you can test and tweak your colours. If you are using gouache or watercolour, you will want to try out different dilutions of ox gall in your paints without muddying your main marbling bath. If you are using acrylics, it is even more important to test your paints to find out which colours disperse more than others.

Controlling colour dispersal with watercolours or gouache

Traditionally, marbling is done using gouache or watercolour paints, which naturally sink under the surface of the size unless you mix a dispersant (ox gall) into them. The more ox gall you add, the further they will spread out on the surface.

METHOD

1 Using an eyedropper or the end of a skewer, place a single drop of paint onto the test bath. It should form a bead and sink into the size.

2 Add a single drop of ox gall to the jar of paint and stir well to combine.

3 Skim the bath with a piece of newspaper to remove the previous paint and repeat step 1. This cleaning process is explained on page 50.

4 Repeat steps 1–3 until the paint floats on the surface of the bath, forming a 5–10cm (2–4in) circle.

5 Repeat steps 1–4 for each of your paints. This may seem tedious but it will help you get good results.

RIGHT Using the thick end of a skewer to place a drop of paint on the size.

Controlling colour dispersal with acrylics

Acrylic paints are more difficult to control than watercolour or gouache as they usually contain a chemical dispersant, meaning many paints will dominate the marbling bath right out of the tube, pushing other colours aside. If you are using acrylics, it is important to test your paints and find out which dominate the most.

METHOD

1 Using a pipette or an eyedropper, place a single drop of paint onto the test bath. It should spread out into a circle.

2 Place a drop of the second colour into the centre of the previous droplet.

3 Continue in this way, with a drop of the third colour in the centre of the second and so on until you've used all your paints, finishing with the first colour you used.

4 Take a look at the size of the rings of colour – are there any that are much larger than the others? Any that are just thin bands?

5 The colours that have the smallest rings will need to be boosted with additional dispersant. For this we can use washing up liquid – but be careful, this is a powerful dispersant that can very easily be too potent! Dilute one part washing up liquid with five parts water and mix well.

6 Add this in small amounts to the paints and test on the test bath each time until you reach a level of dispersal you are happy with.

7 Once you've added dispersant to all the colours that need it, test them together again in your bath. The colours that were previously pushed aside should now be able to hold their own against the more dominant ones.

Many different things affect how much acrylic paint disperses: brand, colour, age of paint and temperature of the size are all factors. It is worth trying out various different types to find ones that work best for you.

Once you start marbling and getting a feel for how the paints behave, feel free to experiment with adding more dispersant to certain paints to get different effects. You might want to mix a colour a little darker than desired, knowing that you will add more dispersant to it and it will expand further, becoming lighter again in the process.

As a general rule, paints are added to the size in order of most dispersion to least dispersion. As each new paint is added, it displaces the previous colour, pushing it back and making it brighter again. This results in an even, bright final paper.

RIGHT Testing the spread of acrylic paints using an eyedropper.

HOW TO MARBLE

Cleaning the size

Before you start marbling and after every impression is taken you must clean the surface of your marbling bath. This removes any particles of dust or paint that might interfere with the pattern.

You can do this with strips of newspaper – simply find the edge of the sheet with a wavy or serrated edge and tear long, straight pieces about 5cm (2in) in width all the way down the paper. Take one of these strips, hold one end against the left inside edge of your bath, and 'measure' the length of the bath against the strip. Tear off any excess and you should have a strip that fits perfectly inside your bath.

Hold the strip between your thumb and fingers at either end. Make sure it is taut, then place it onto your size at a 45-degree angle and pull it towards you. This should catch all the dust, bubbles and old paint that has collected on the size. I always keep a rubbish bin close at hand to put these pieces into.

Applying paint

There are different ways of applying paint to the size that give many varied effects. Marbling rewards spontaneity, so be sure to experiment with different ones or try combining them. The most commonly used methods are using a stiff brush, an eyedropper or a rake. You can make your own rake following the instructions on page 58.

RIGHT Applying paint strategically using an eyedropper.

Using a stiff brush

Traditional Turkish marbling is performed with a brush made of horsehair bundled together and tied around a rosewood stick. The stiff bristles allow for a sprinkling of smaller drops of paint evenly across the surface of the bath. You can also use a standard round stiff-bristle brush or, for a more rustic feel, a bundle of broom straw tied together with string.

Using this method is a great way to get quick, even coverage. Stir the paint with your brush, saturating it thoroughly. Then, holding it over your marbling bath at a distance of 20–30cm (8–12in), tap it against a finger on your non-dominant hand (or metal rod) to deposit paint. Keep your hands moving over the bath to make sure you get an even coverage of paint. Larger brushes will produce larger drops.

A traditional pattern called Turkish Spot can be achieved with this method, starting with the colour that disperses the most and finishing with the colour that disperses the least, for a beautiful effect with areas of clustered colours.

LEFT A collection of stiff-bristle paintbrushes suitable for use when marbling.

Using a pipette or eyedropper

Use an eyedropper or pipette to control exactly where you want to place colour on the marbling bath. Eyedroppers are good for releasing a drop of paint at a time for a very controlled pattern, although you'll need to keep going back for more paint.

Fight the urge to release the bulb after each drop – you'll suck air into the pipette or eyedropper which will make your paint bubble up. It's best to fill it with a few drops and maintain a steady pressure between drops.

This method is good for very regular patterns or for placing drops of colour in strategic places – however, it does take much longer to get a good coverage of paint using only this method.

ABOVE Dropping paint on the size in regular lines using an eyedropper.

Rakes and combs

European marbling features the use of a variety of rakes and fine-toothed combs to make intricate patterns in the paint once it is on the bath. These can also be used to insert lines of colour onto the size – which is good for repeat patterns.

Rakes made of wooden dowels are good for thick lines of colour as they hold a lot of paint, though thinner wire combs can be used, too, for smaller bands of colour. Apply paint evenly onto the tines using a brush. You could experiment by using different colours on different parts of the rake, or even mixing colours for an ombré effect. Don't apply so much that the paint drips before you can manoeuvre it into the right place on the bath though!

Carefully move the rake to the place on the bath you'd like to use it, holding it with tines pointing upwards if you are worried about dripping, and then gently place the tines onto the surface of the bath, letting the paint disperse until you're happy with it (see photographs opposite).

LEFT If you apply paint with a rake and then create a combed pattern (see page 107), the resulting pattern will have a pleasingly ordered feel.

RIGHT Applying paint in lines using a rake.

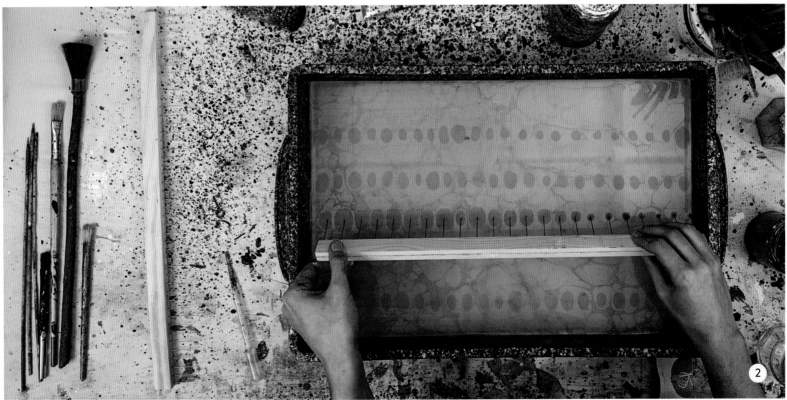

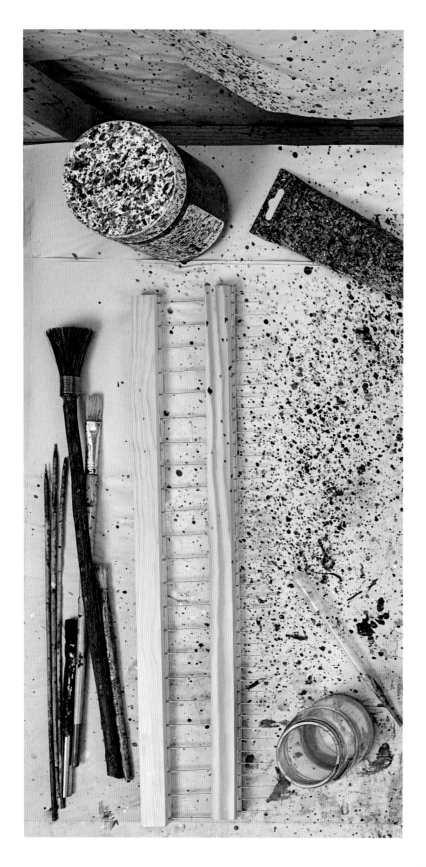

How to make a comb

Combs and rakes form a large part of Europe's marbling tradition. They are exactly how they sound: long metal- or wood-toothed combs that can be pulled through the size to create intricate, uniform patterns.

Marbling combs are not commonly available items so it is often easiest to make them yourself. This has the added benefits of them fitting perfectly in your bath, plus you can control exactly how widely the teeth are spaced and how thick the teeth are, or you can design them according to a particular pattern you want to make. The thicker the width of the teeth, the more the paint will move on the size. You may wish to make two combs, one to fit the length and the other the width of your marbling bath.

Tip

You can also make rudimentary combs by cutting bamboo skewers into smaller pieces and hot-gluing them to a piece of corrugated cardboard, or by hammering nails at regular intervals into a piece of soft balsa wood.

WHAT YOU NEED

- 5cm (2in) upholstery pins (these have a T-shaped head)
- 2 pieces of wood, 30cm (12in) wide x 2cm (¾in) high x 0.5cm (¼in) deep
- Strong wood or general-purpose adhesive
- Pencil
- Glue spreader or brush
- 3 clamps or strong clips
- Ruler or tape measure

METHOD

1 Lay one of the pieces of wood flat on a table with one of the 30 x 2cm (12 x ¾in) faces uppermost. Make pencil marks at 2cm (¾in) intervals along the length of the wood, leaving 1cm at either end. Extend these pencil lines down the width of the wood, ensuring they are all parallel.

2 Spread glue generously over the wood, ensuring you can still see the pencil lines.

3 Press upholstery pins into the glue, with their heads within the wood section and the sharp ends facing outwards. Try to arrange the pins so they sit on and continue the lines you have drawn on the wood.

4 Press the second piece of wood onto the glued pins so they are sandwiched between two pieces of wood. Make sure the pins are straight and parallel to each other.

5 Place clamps along the length of the comb and leave to dry for 24 hours.

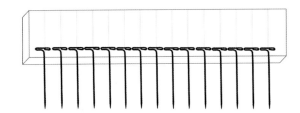

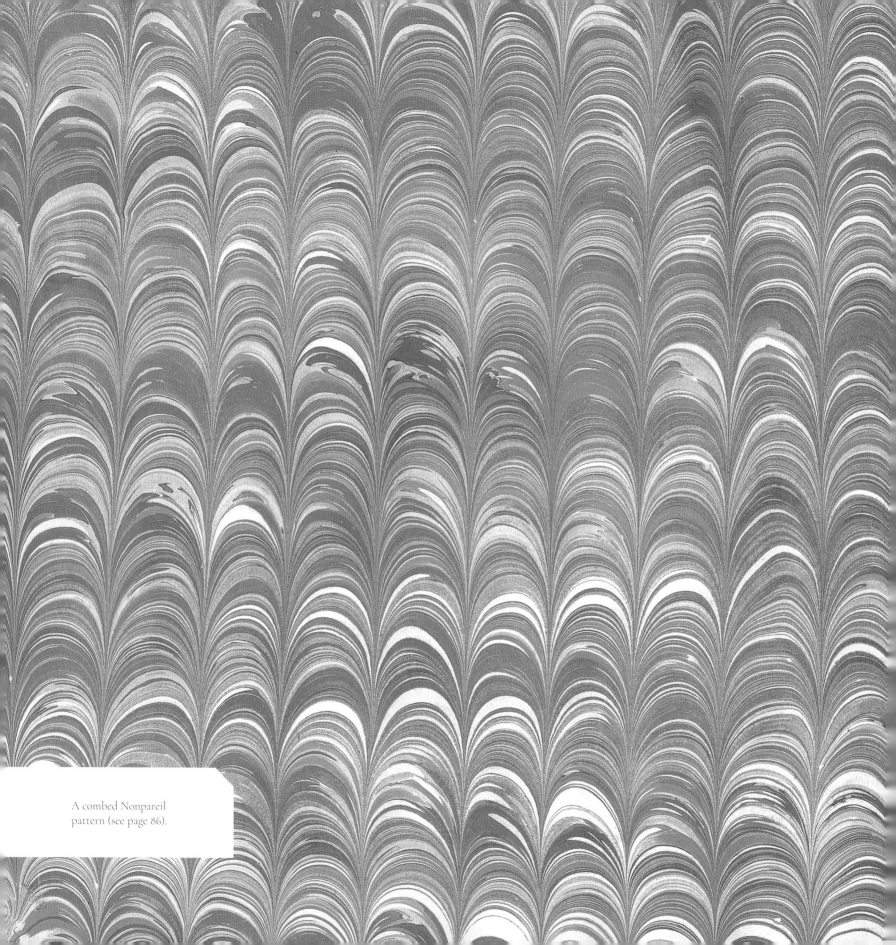

A combed Nonpareil
pattern (see page 86).

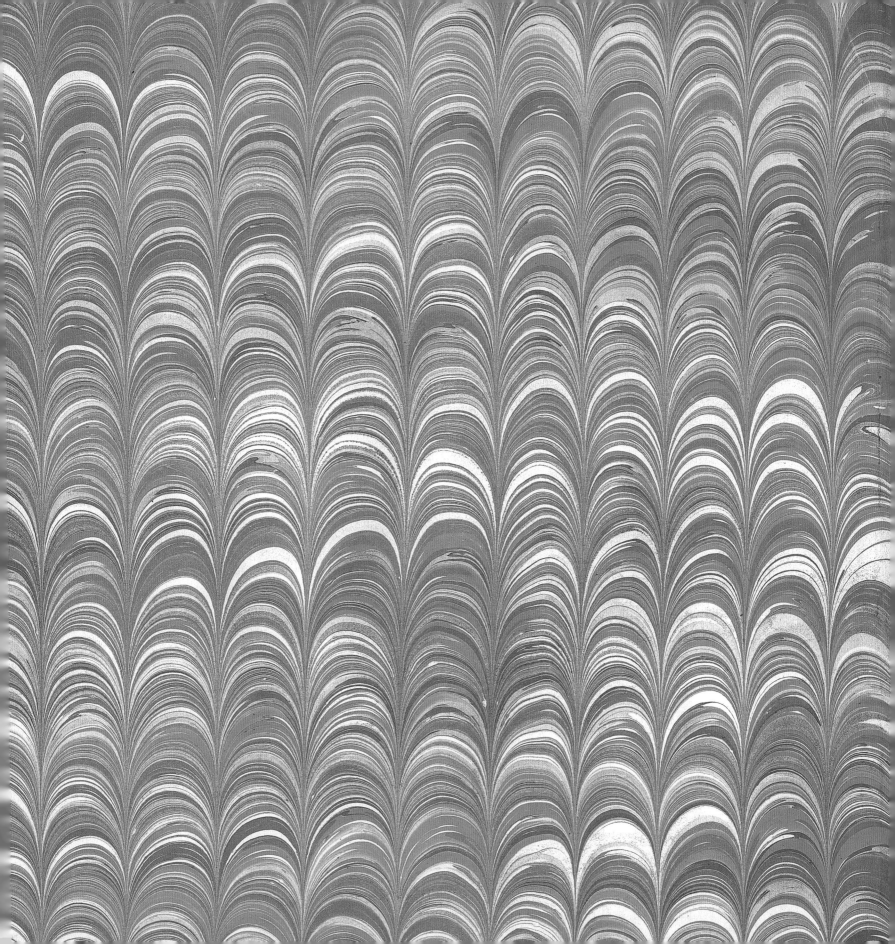

How to lay the paper

Capturing the pattern onto a piece of paper is probably the trickiest part of marbling to master – be prepared for a fair few strange lines and air bubbles before you start achieving consistently clear prints. Check out the troubleshooting tips on pages 135–139 for further guidance if you are having difficulties. As with all things marbling, practice makes perfect – don't give up!

When you are happy with your pattern and ready to transfer it to paper, it's time to remove the weight from your stack of previously mordanted papers (see pages 30–31) and peel off the first sheet. Try not to disturb the rest of the stack and keep them under a plastic sheet so they retain their moisture and flexibility.

Remember to check that you can see the X marking the back of your paper – this is crucial, otherwise you could end up marbling the un-mordanted side.

Hold the paper at diagonally opposite corners and give it a couple of rippling shakes to make sure it is flexible and supple – don't hold it taut.

Lower the corner that you're holding that's closer to you onto the surface of the size. As soon as it touches the surface, slowly bring your other hand down, allowing the paper to lower onto the size until the whole piece is laying upon it. Do not move the hand closest to you during this process – if necessary rest your hand or wrist on the side of the bath to keep it as steady as possible. Once the entire paper is on the size, it is safe to take your hands away.

LEFT Laying the paper carefully onto the marbling bath.

ABOVE Peeling the marbled paper from the surface of the size.

This should be a single fluid but controlled motion – make sure you don't pause or jerk the paper (this causes lines in the pattern) or drop it, trapping air between the paper and surface of the size, causing air bubbles that show up as blobs of white, disrupting your pattern.

Once the paper is laying on the size, be careful as it is more delicate when wet. Hold the two corners furthest from you in the bath and gently peel the paper up from the surface towards you. If you know which way the grain of your paper runs, it's easiest to peel it up in line with the grain.

Transfer the paper onto a rigid board or metal sheet bigger than the paper. Keep this close to the bath to minimize dripping.

Rinsing and drying

It's important to rinse your papers after marbling them to wash off any size residue and excess paint. It will also hugely decrease the drying time, as carrageenan residue left on the paper clings to it and prevents airflow from drying it out.

Drying times will vary based on the ambient temperature, amount of draught and paper absorbency. It usually takes around an hour for a properly rinsed paper to become fully dry.

Set up a rinsing station in a large sink or a deep container – use a thick sheet of metal, plastic or sealed wood that is larger than the size of your paper, propped at an angle within your sink or tray. You could also use the board you placed the paper on straight after marbling. Carry your freshly marbled paper on your board to the rinsing station and drape it carefully on the angled surface, making sure to avoid creasing it.

Fill a 5 litre (10 pint) jug or 8 litre (14 pint) hand-pumped sprayer with water and pour or spray evenly over the entirety of your paper. If using a sprayer, the pressure can be quite high so be sure to hold the nozzle about 30cm (12in) away from the paper – the paint on freshly marbled paper has not set and can be easily smudged or disturbed, so be careful when handling it.

Gingerly lift your paper from the rinsing sheet and take it to your drying area, which can be a washing line or a household airer. Hang your paper using plastic pegs to hold it in place in the top corners. If using an airer, make sure to hang your first papers at the top and work downwards so subsequent ones won't drip onto them. If drying your papers inside, you may want to lay a sheet of plastic underneath to protect the floor from water and paint residue.

Flattening your papers

Once your papers are fully dry, you will find they have warped and are quite stiff. This is completely normal – paper fibres expand when wet and shrink again as they dry, causing them to lose their shape when they dry unevenly.

It's easy to fix this: stack your dry papers into a pile, then place them between a flat surface and a large, heavy book. Leave them overnight and they should be much flatter and more pliable the next morning. If you have a book press, this does the job very well.

LEFT Rinsing the freshly-marbled paper.

BASIC PATTERNS

Making patterns

The beauty of marbling is in the chaos of it. There is only so much control that we can have over the movement of the paint on the size so it is impossible to make the same paper twice: similar, perhaps, but never the same. Every single paper is a unique piece. The possibilities are endless! It's an exciting, and slightly overwhelming, realization.

Over the centuries, master marblers developed their own techniques and ways of manipulating the size which became established patterns. To help open up some of the possibilities of marbling, I will guide you through a few of the simplest patterns that form the basis of many more complex designs. These include the Nonpareil, shown opposite, and a few freestyle patterns like hearts (see page 92) and flowers (see page 94).

I suggest trying them out a few times, perhaps with different colours, to get a feel for the way the paint behaves and how small variations in your movements can change the pattern.

RIGHT A finely combed
Nonpareil (see page 86).

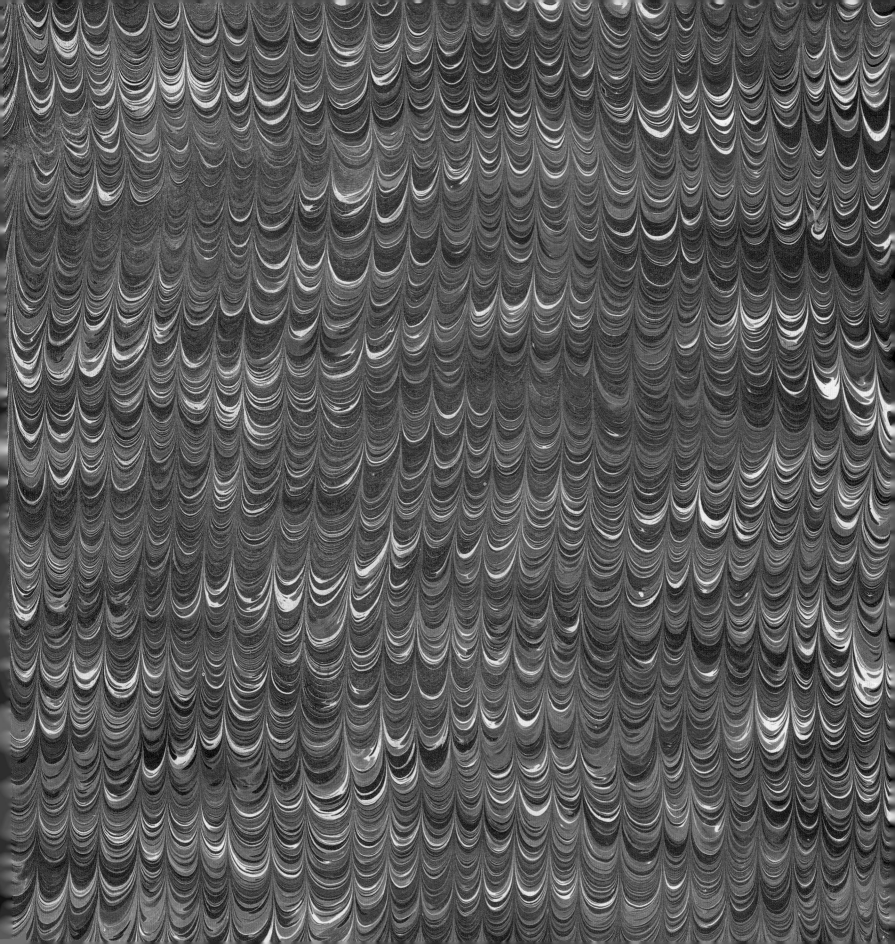

Stone

Perhaps the simplest pattern to achieve, Stone gives a beautiful
naturalistic effect much like the marble after which the craft is named.

WHAT YOU'LL NEED

Size bath (see page 23)
4–6 prepared paint colours (see page 26)
Paintbrushes
Mordanted paper (see pages 29–31)

METHOD

1 Think about which colour you would like to form the veins (the thin lines in between larger areas of colour). This colour needs to be applied first. Using a paintbrush, sprinkle the surface of the size evenly with your first colour.

2 Apply the second colour evenly over the surface of the bath. You will notice that the first colour starts to be pushed back into the beginnings of veins. Your second colour should disperse easily. If you find it is making small circles – 3cm (1¼in) or less, add some dispersant to it to give some more spread (see page 46).

3 Continue adding paints to the size, building up the colours. Each subsequent colour should disperse slightly less than the previous one to create a pleasant, even effect.

4 When you have added all the colours, your first colour should have been pushed into thin veins. You may want to lightly sprinkle more of this first colour over your size if you feel there isn't enough of it left – or, alternatively, consider using a complementary colour as a final addition for a visual 'pop'.

5 Lay your paper carefully onto the bath to pick up your pattern.

6 Remove, rinse and hang to dry (see page 65).

Experimenting with the pattern

Try mixing up the order in which you put the paints on: use the strongest-dispersing paint last. How does this affect the final pattern? Note how this changes the tone of the colour compared to when you put it on previously.

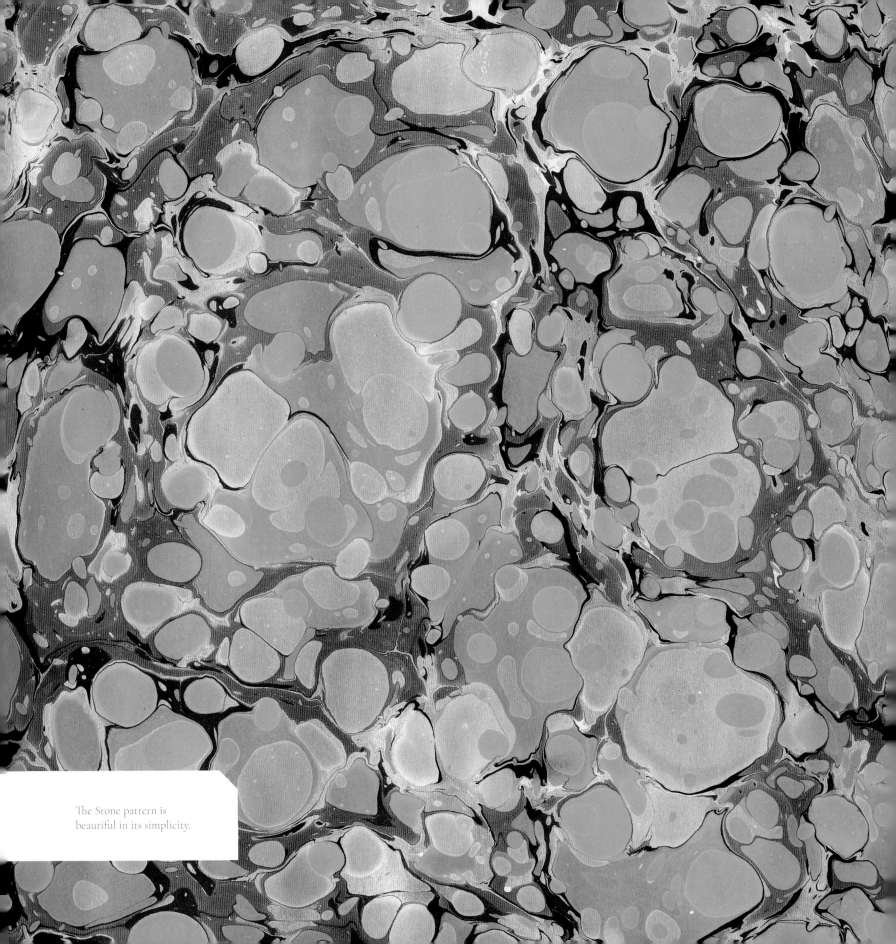

The Stone pattern is
beautiful in its simplicity.

Swirl

This is a great beginner's pattern as it's easy and very elegant. In this pattern, we introduce our first tool: the stylus. This could be a skewer, knitting needle or even the end of your paintbrush. Notice how it pulls the paint into fluid shape in its wake.

Be careful not to overdo the process, as too much swirling can make the pattern confused and muddy.

WHAT YOU'LL NEED

Size bath (see page 23)
4–6 prepared paint colours (see page 26)
Stylus (skewer, knitting needle or similar)
Mordanted paper (see pages 29–31)

METHOD

1 Follow the instructions for making a Stone pattern (see page 70), stopping before you lay your paper onto the bath.

2 Insert your stylus and into the size.

3 Move your stylus freely around in curved, sweeping motions. It's okay to take the stylus out of the size and insert it elsewhere. Try making spirals and S-shapes.

4 Lay your paper carefully onto the bath to pick up your pattern.

5 Remove, rinse and hang to dry (see page 65).

Changing the stylus

Use a thinner stylus, such as a needle. How does the thinner width affect the way the paint is pulled over the size? Does it create more or less movement? Try again with the end of a large paintbrush – what effect does this thicker implement have?

Freestyle Swirl patterns really show off the fluidity of the technique.

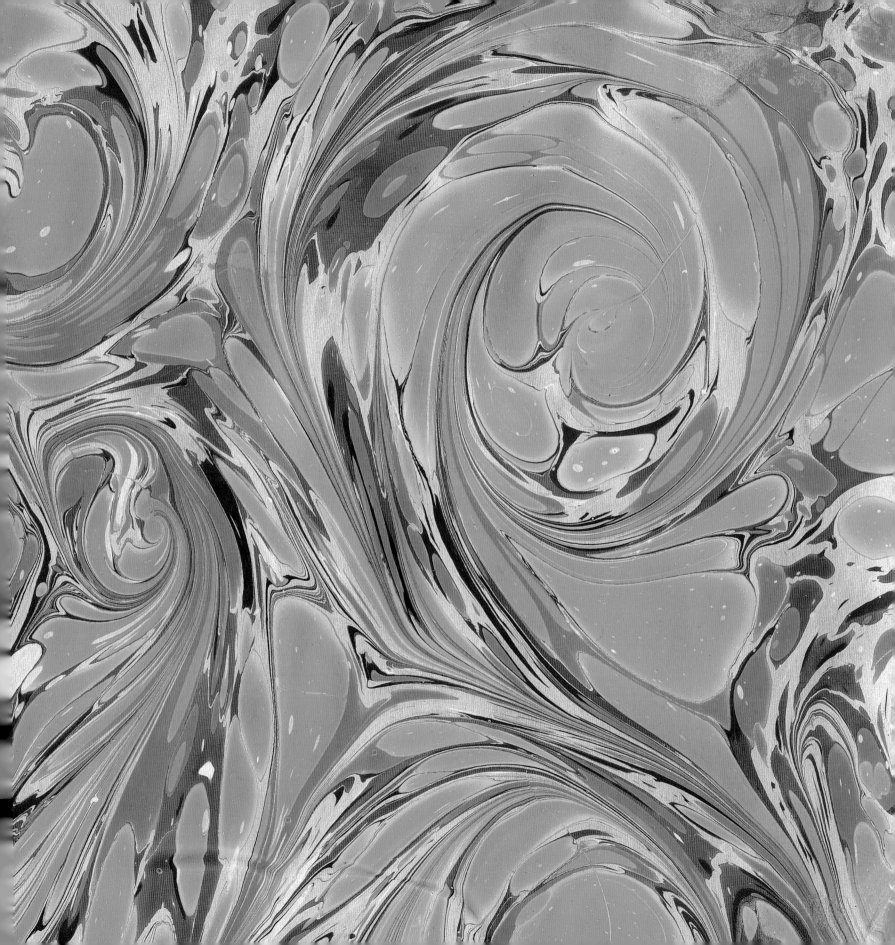

Git-gel

This is one of the rudimentary patterns of the Turkish tradition and the first step of most combed patterns. The word 'git-gel' has a similar meaning to 'zig-zag' – for obvious reasons! The purpose of this pattern is to re-shape the paint from blobs into long, thin bands of colour.

WHAT YOU'LL NEED

Size bath (see page 23)
4–6 prepared paint colours (see page 26)
Stylus – a skewer works well
Mordanted paper (see pages 29–31)

Watch out

Try to keep the zig-zag lines as close to each other as you can, but avoid going over a previously drawn line in the size – it will make a loop shape that is difficult to fix. It is best to go slowly at first so you can control the pattern.

METHOD

1 Apply each colour in turn using a paintbrush, as you would for the Stone pattern (see page 70). Add dispersant to your paints as needed so that they disperse evenly – there shouldn't be any dominant colours.

2 Insert your stylus into the size at the top corner.

3 Drag it straight along the top of the bath to the opposite corner.

4 Pull it through the size to the other side of the bath, aiming for a point around 2cm (¾in) below the place you started.

5 Repeat step 4, pulling the skewer to the other side.

6 Repeat steps 4 and 5 until you reach the bottom of the bath.

7 Lay your paper carefully onto the bath to pick up your pattern.

8 Remove, rinse and hang out to dry (see page 65).

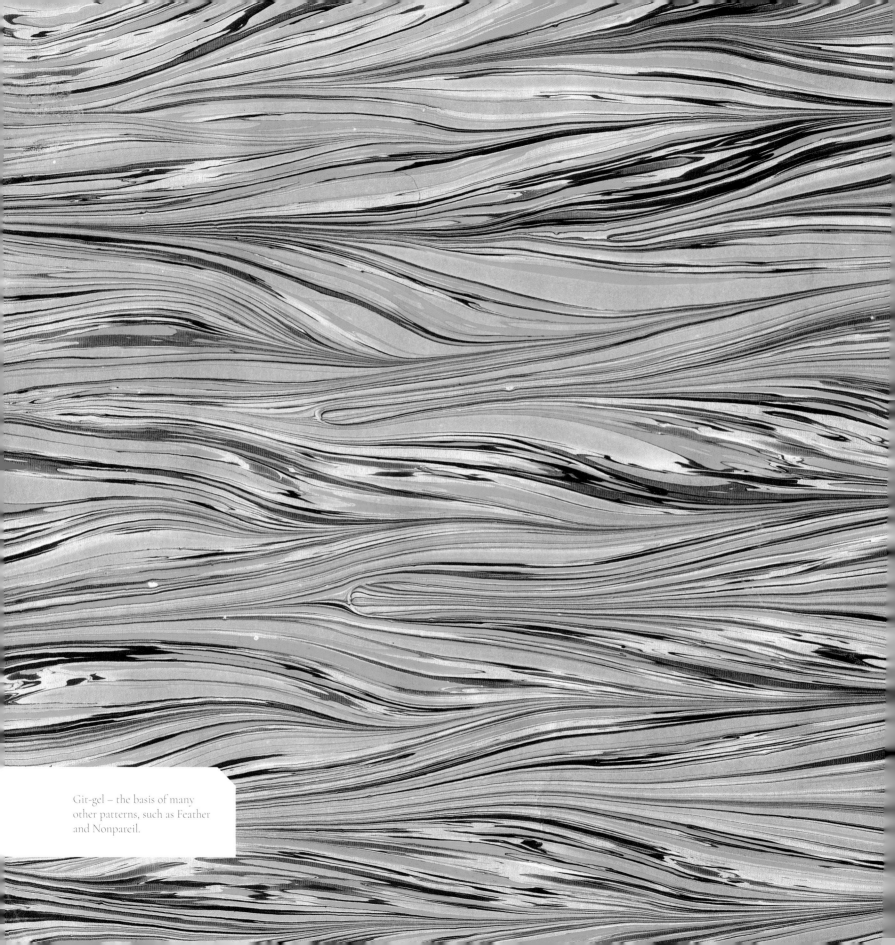

Git-gel – the basis of many
other patterns, such as Feather
and Nonpareil.

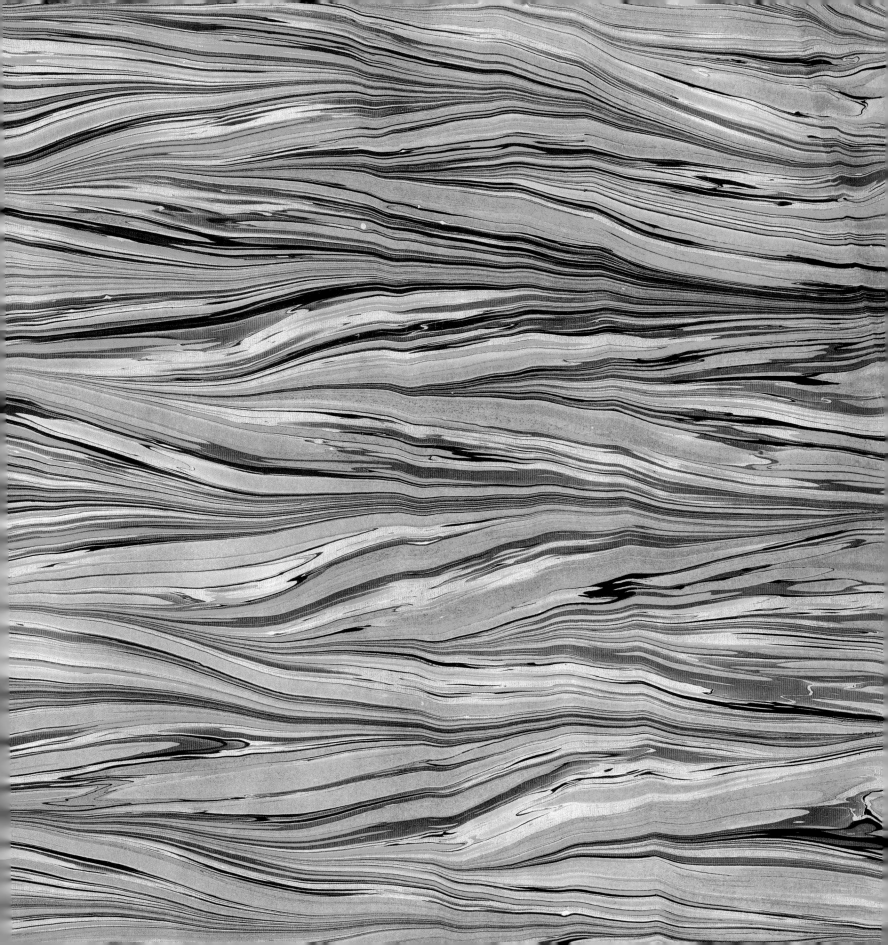

Feather

A variation on the git-gel, this expressive pattern resembles interlocking feathers.

WHAT YOU'LL NEED

Size bath (see page 23)
4–6 prepared paint colours (see page 26)
Paintbrushes
Stylus (skewer, knitting needle or similar)
Mordanted paper (see pages 29–31)

METHOD

1 Apply each colour one after the other using a paintbrush as you would for the Stone pattern (see page 70).

2 Insert your stylus at the very top of the bath, about 2.5cm (1in) to the right of the left-hand corner.

3 Bring the stylus down diagonally to a point about 2.5cm (1in) below the left-hand corner, forming a triangle shape with the corner of the bath.

4 Drag the stylus down the left edge of the bath for about 5cm (2in).

5 Move the stylus diagonally up to the top edge of the bath, making sure to keep the motion parallel to your first diagonal line.

6 Drag the stylus along the top edge of the bath for about 5cm (2in).

7 Repeat the motions in steps 3–6, keeping the lines parallel, until you have travelled across the bath to the diagonally opposite corner.

8 Lay your paper carefully onto the bath to pick up your pattern (see page 62–63.

9 Remove, rinse and hang out to dry (see page 65).

Adapting the pattern

Instead of making straight-line movements, try making wavy lines as you create the feather shapes in the size. How does this affect the pattern?

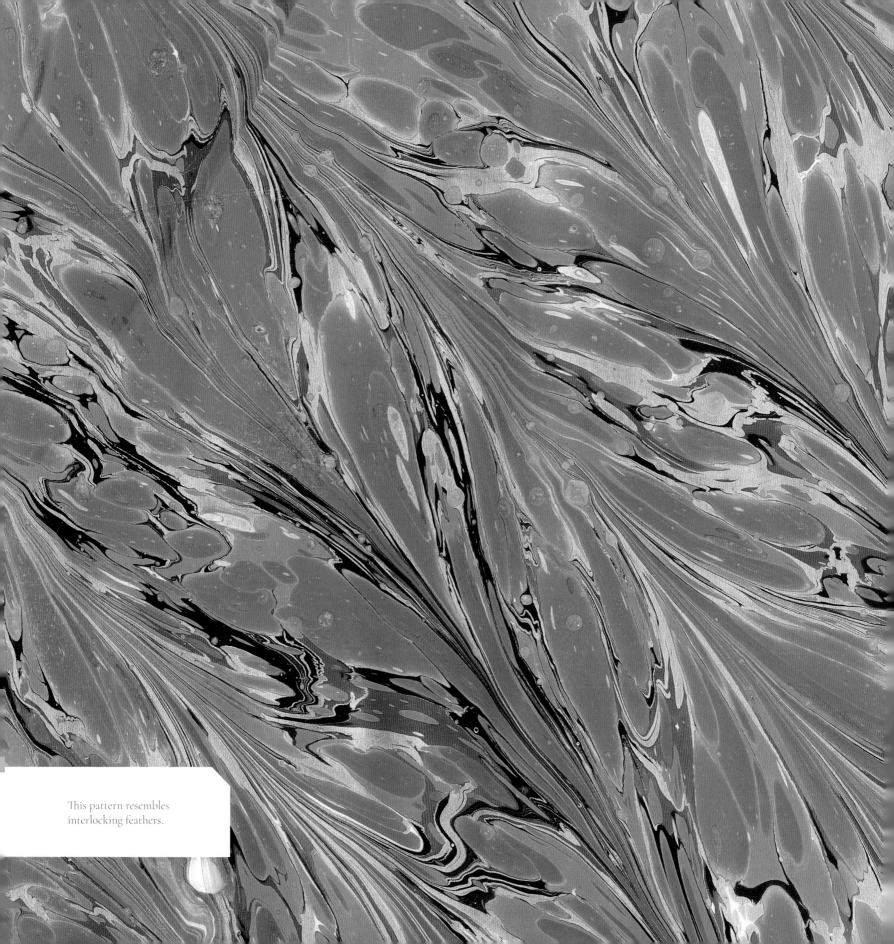

This pattern resembles
interlocking feathers.

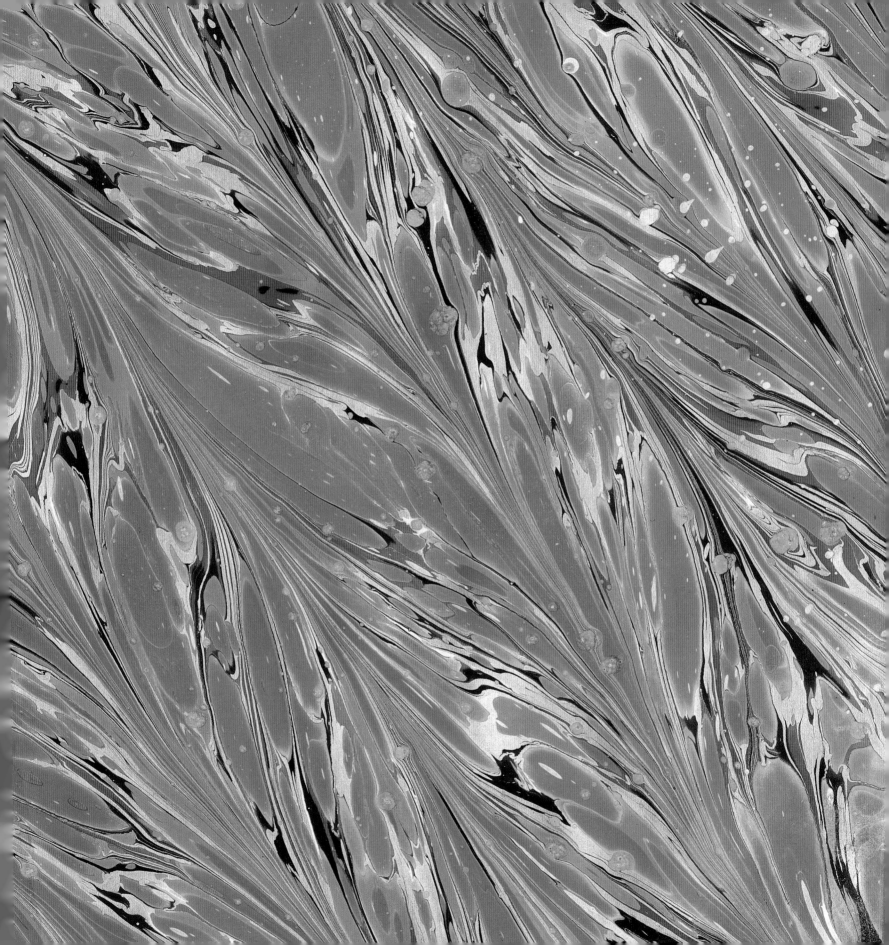

Nonpareil

This is a French pattern, as suggested by its name, which means 'unparalleled' (ironic, considering it is characterized by parallel lines!). Dating back to the early seventeenth century, it is a combed pattern, built on top of a git-gel, that completely transforms the character of the colours you are using. I recommend using five or more colours to get a good effect.

Traditionally, Nonpareil was performed with a very fine-toothed comb, but you can use a variety of combs or rakes to create your own twists on this pattern (see page 58 on making your own combs).

WHAT YOU'LL NEED

Size bath (see page 23)
5–6 prepared paint colours (see page 26)
Stylus – a skewer works well
Comb or rake
Mordanted paper (see pages 29–31)

METHOD

1 Follow the instructions for making a Stone pattern (see page 70), stopping before you lay your paper onto the bath. You will want to make sure your colours are as evenly represented as possible on the bath so, if necessary, add a little more of any colours that have been pushed back into veins.

2 Use your stylus to make a git-gel (see page 78), ensuring that you move the stylus perpendicular to the direction you want the nonpareil lines to go (if you wanted the nonpareil lines to be parallel to the long sides of the bath, you would move the stylus back and forth parallel to the short sides of the bath for the git-gel).

3 Insert your comb carefully at the top or side of your bath (depending on the direction of your git-gel), at a 45-degree angle.

4 Slowly and smoothly pull the comb through the bath, being careful not to let the handle dip into the size.

5 Lay your paper carefully onto the bath to pick up your pattern.

6 Remove, rinse and hang to dry (see page 65).

Adapting the pattern

Try sprinkling an accent colour on top of the finished Nonpareil to break the regularity. I don't like patterns to be too 'perfect'! Their irregularities add interest and keep them contemporary.

This Nonpareil was
created using a comb
made with thin wire teeth.

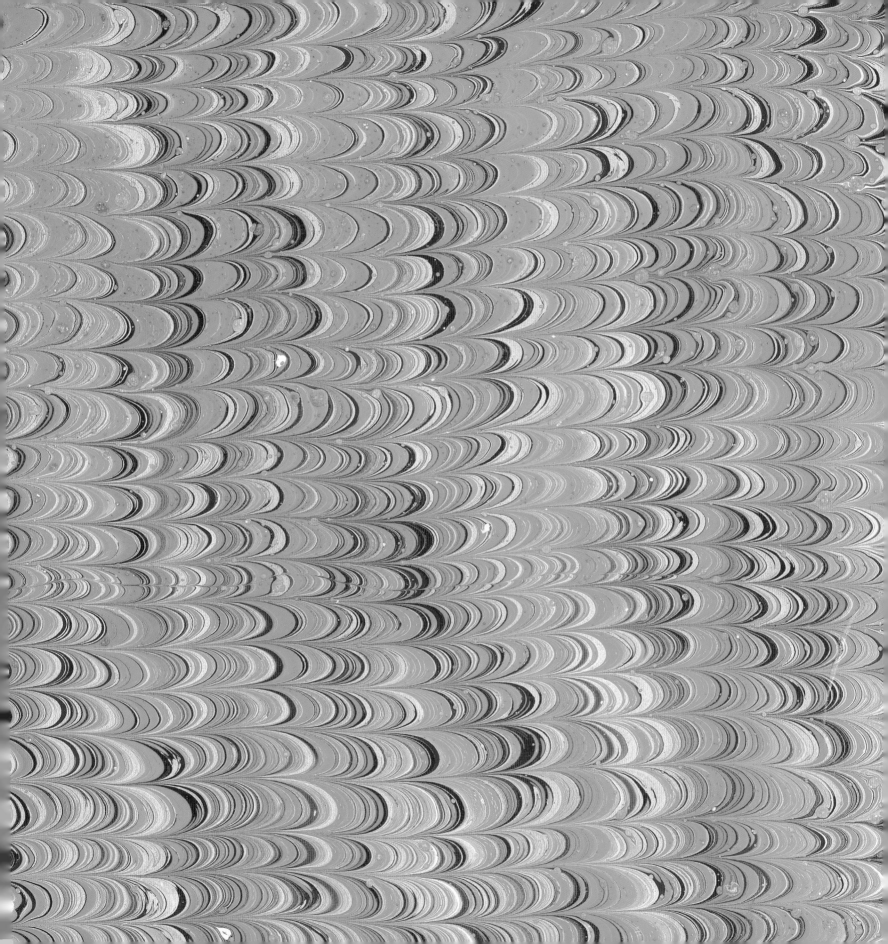

Ebru – painting on water

Marbling originated in Turkey, and it is still a large part of Turkish culture. In 2014, it was recognised as a UNESCO Intangible Cultural Heritage of Humanity to be protected. Marbling, called *ebru* in Turkish, is considered a stand-alone art form, with many master marblers creating beautiful, intricate paintings of flowers in their marbling baths. It takes a lot of skill and patience to paint on water at this level, but there are a few simple designs that also produce very pleasing results.

Bullseyes

If you flip back to page 46, I described how to test the dispersal level of your paints by making circles of paint inside each other. This is essentially all you do to make the simplest form of *ebru*, a bullseye. A single, large bullseye in the centre of a detailed combed pattern can be a very effective way to disrupt it, making a bold artistic statement.

METHOD

1 Using an eyedropper or the blunt end of a skewer, place a single drop of paint onto the bath. It should spread out into a circle.

2 Place a drop of the next colour into the centre of the previous droplet.

3 Continue adding to the bullseye with other colours until you are happy with the effect.

LEFT if you have the patience, you can create all kinds of images in your marbling bath – such as this galloping horse.

RIGHT Making bullseyes with a bamboo skewer.

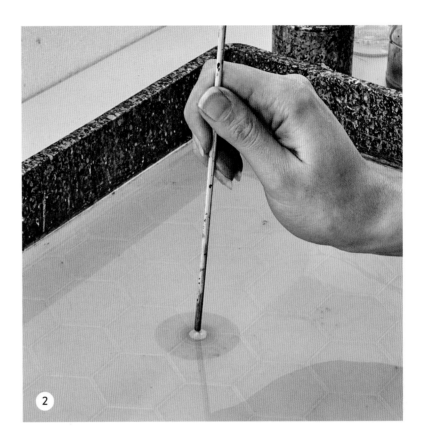

Heart

This simple variation of a bullseye is a lot of fun. Make a single large heart as shown in the demonstration, or lots of smaller ones as shown opposite. A single heart could be used for a card or even transferred onto fabric (see page 123).

METHOD

1 Make a bullseye as described on page 91.

2 Insert the pointed end of your skewer into the size just above the top of the bullseye.

3 Pull the skewer straight down through the whole bullseye, and continue a little further to make the tail of the heart.

LEFT The process of making a heart.

RIGHT A patterned paper using repeated heart motifs.

Flower

METHOD

1 Make a bullseye as described on page 91.

2 Insert the pointed end of your skewer into the size just above the top of the bullseye, at the 12 o'clock mark if it were a clock.

3 Pull the skewer into the centre of the bullseye and gently remove.

4 Insert the skewer at the 2 o'clock position of the bullseye and repeat step 3.

5 Continue this technique, inserting the skewer at even points around the 'clockface' of the bullseye.

ABOVE Once you have mastered the basic technique, you can experiment with different shapes and designs.

RIGHT The process for making a flower with rounded petals as described in the steps.

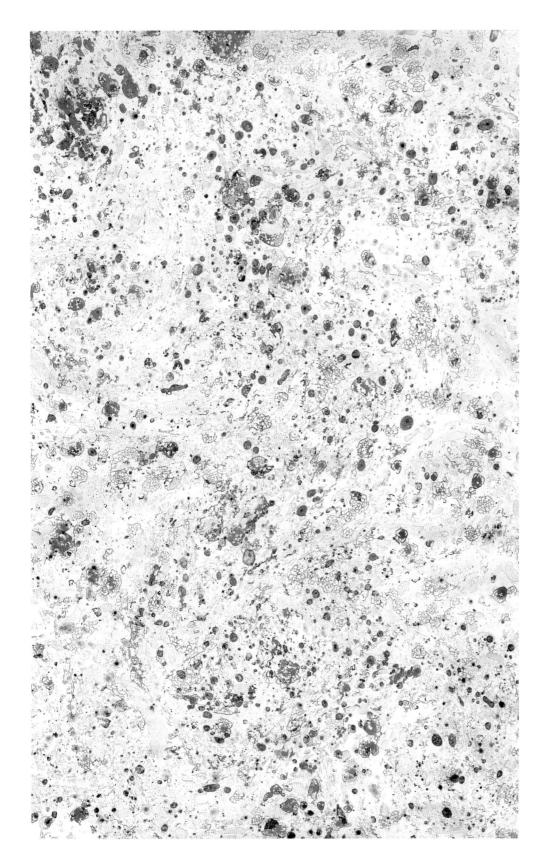

Marbling with oil paints

Oil paints are interesting because they are naturally hydrophobic – meaning that they will float on top of water without the need to thicken it first. Using plain water does have its downsides though – when anything disrupts the water's surface, it causes lots of chaotic movement that makes it impossible to make controlled patterns like the ones previously described. The hydrophobic quality of oil paints also causes them to bead up on the surface rather than spreading out in smooth swathes.

This is still a very beautiful and interesting effect, though – and as contemporary marbling starts to move away from the more traditional, precise patterns, I think it's definitely worth experimenting with.

LEFT Oil paint can bead and fragment as it spreads out due to its hydrophobic nature.

RIGHT The swirls in this piece were creating by drawing through the bath with a skewer.

1 You don't need to mordant paper when using oil paints, so just set your paper aside ready to use. Make sure your paper is supple and flexible as it won't be benefiting from the dampness of the mordant.

2 Use either plain water (filtered or distilled is best) or a thin carrageenan size – 1 litre (1¾ pints) mixed with distilled or filtered water).

3 Mix your oil paints with turpentine to thin them to the consistency of water.

4 Flick the paints onto the surface of the water or size as you would normally. They should float and spread out.

5 Blow on the surface of the water to move the colours around, or use a skewer to stir them gently.

6 Lay a piece of paper carefully onto the surface to pick up the paint.

7 Hang to dry without rinsing. Oil paints take a longer time to dry than gouache or acrylics, so resist the urge to touch!

Safety information

Make sure you try this in a well-ventilated room – turpentine emits hazardous fumes that should not be inhaled.

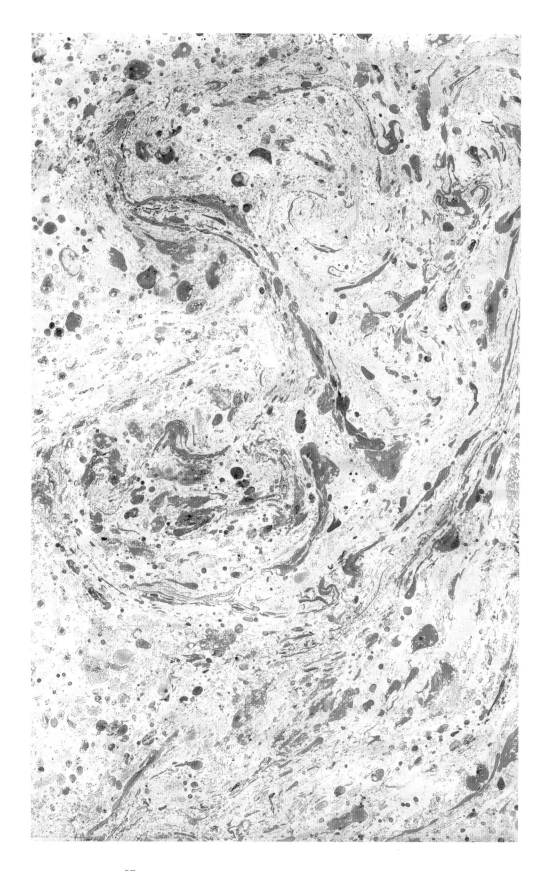

ADVANCED TECHNIQUES

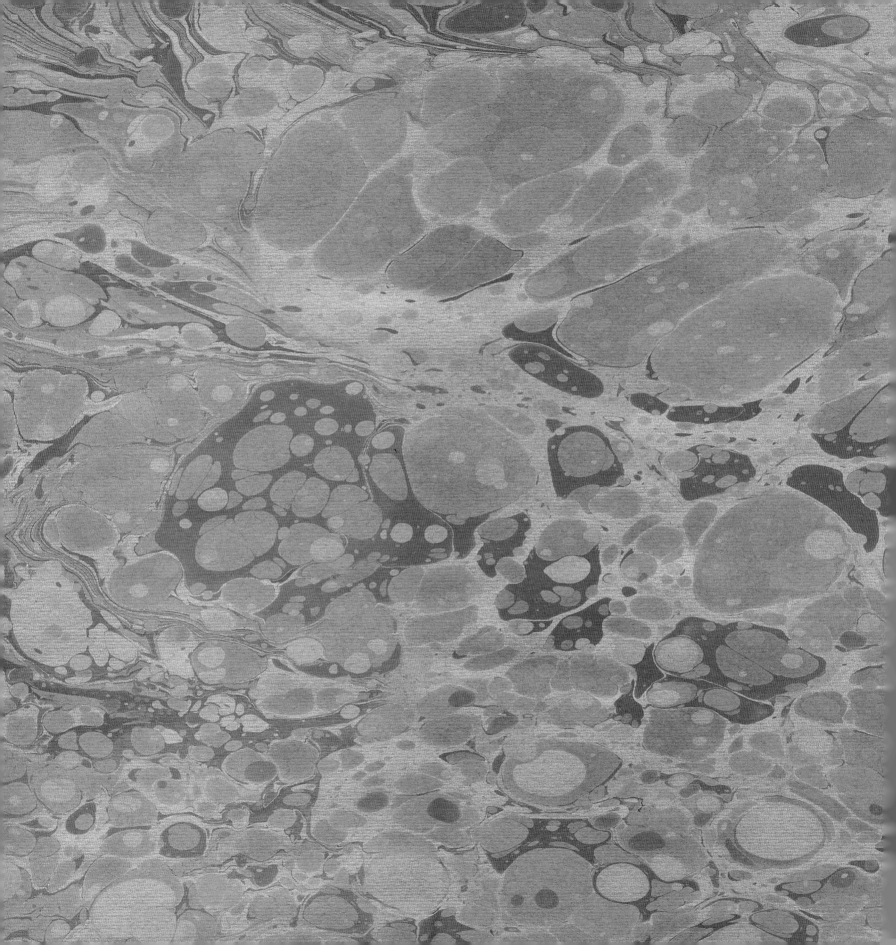

Using coloured paper

A simple and exciting way to push your marbling is to experiment with the paper you marble onto – using a coloured paper will affect the way more transparent paints appear and completely change the character of your papers.

Dispersant as colour

Dispersant is very useful for controlling the spread of your paints – but it can also be used straight on the marbling bath for some great effects. It acts as an 'invisible' paint, creating holes in the pattern where it hits the size. This can be particularly effective if you are using a coloured or printed paper as a base, as it allows the base colour to come through.

Using paper that has been pre-painted with watercolour washes

Don't be afraid to combine other techniques with marbling. Watercolour washes can create beautiful soft colour gradients, which add a lovely dimension to marbled papers. Just be careful when mordanting your painted paper!

LEFT A delicate Stone pattern on a dusty rose coloured paper.

RIGHT All these papers were created using exactly the same paints – it's just the colour of the paper that has changed.

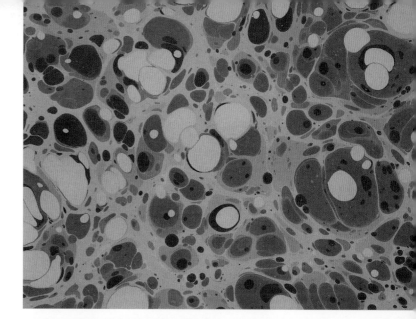

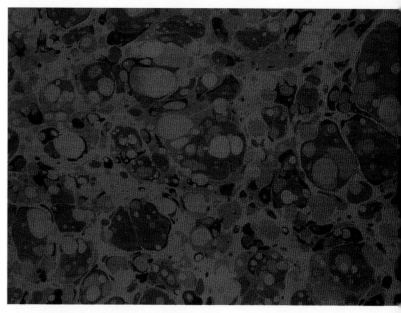

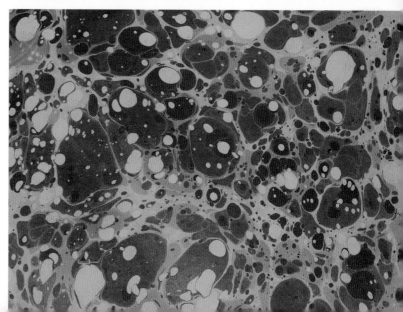

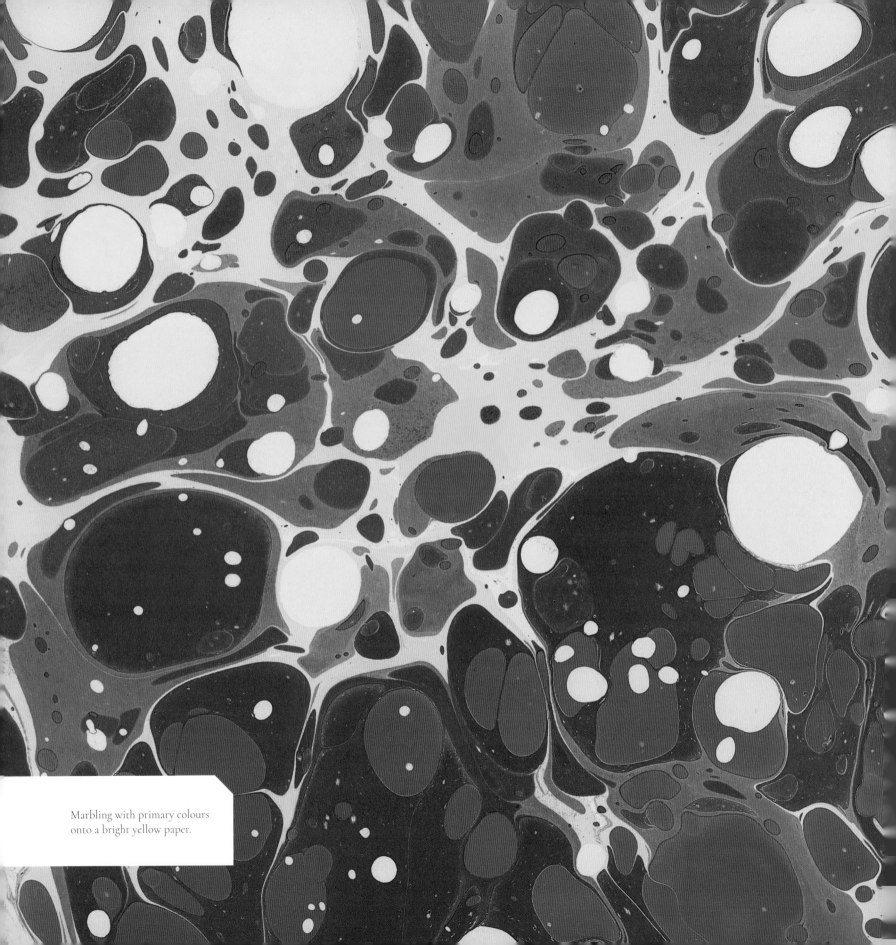

Marbling with primary colours onto a bright yellow paper.

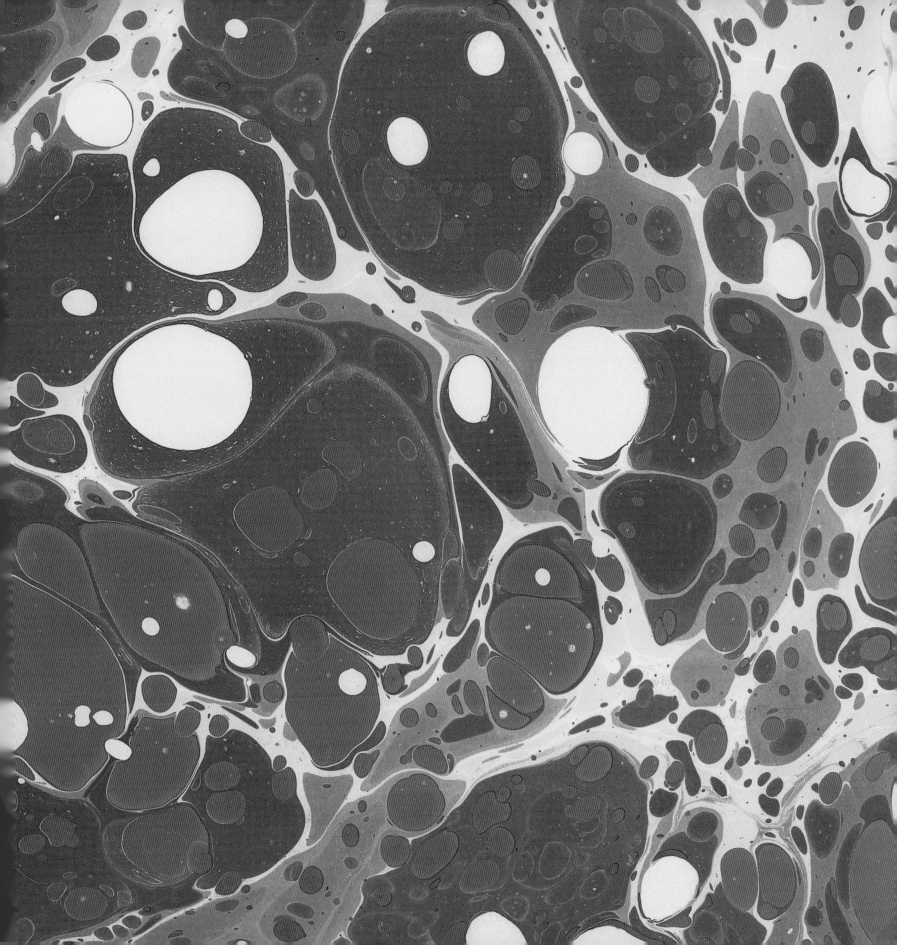

Combed patterns

French Curl

1 This requires an additional step to the Nonpareil (see page 86). First, make a Stone pattern as explained on page 70.

2 Turn it into a git-gel as on page 78.

3 Comb it to make a Nonpareil as on page 86.

4 Once you have completed your Nonpareil design on the size, take a skewer and draw neat little spirals at regular points throughout the pattern.

LEFT A French Curl
in blue tones.

RIGHT The process
of making a French
Curl pattern.

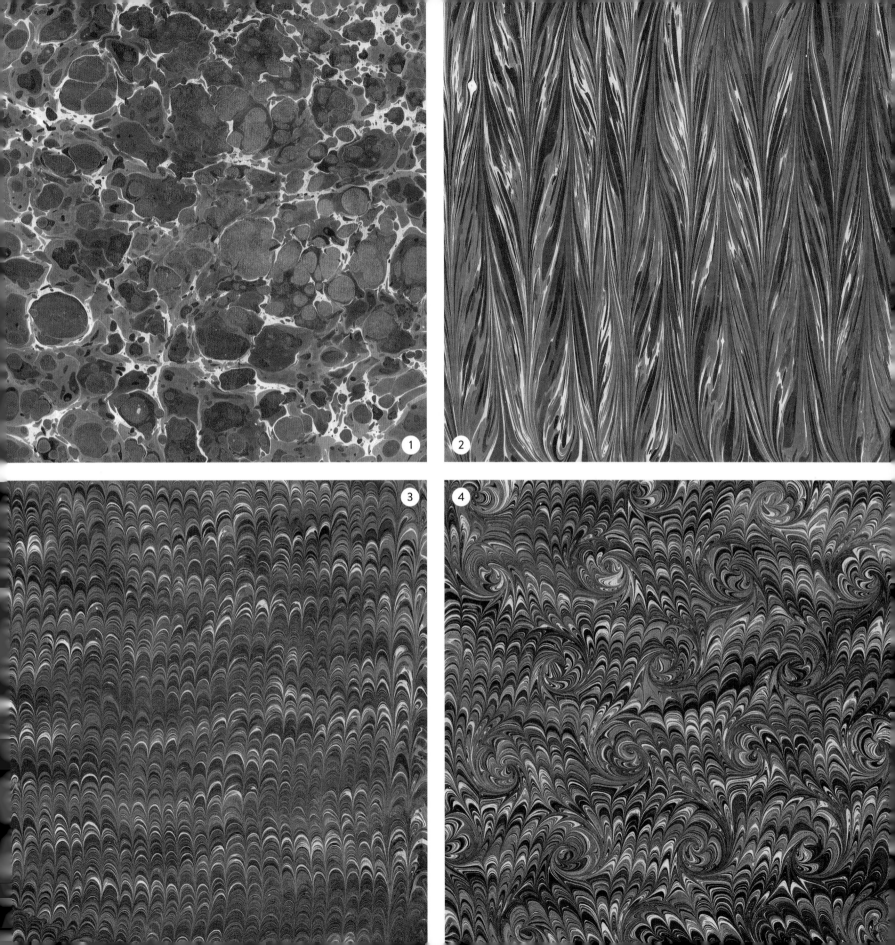

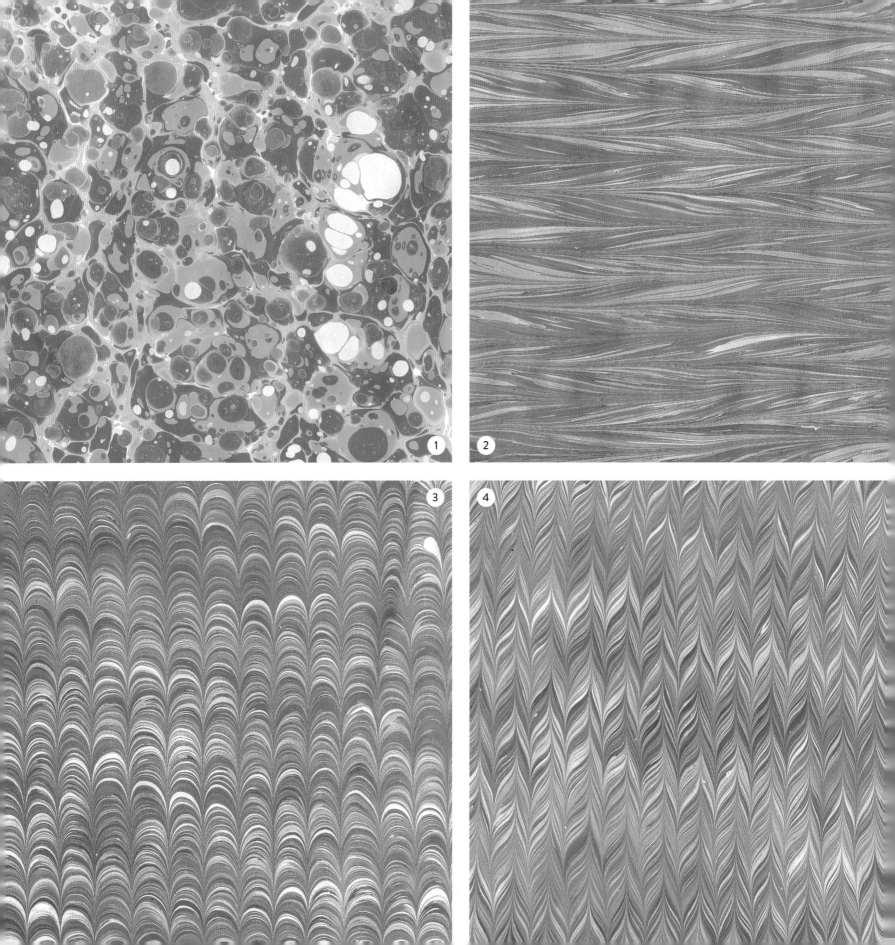

Chevron

1 Make a Stone pattern as explained on page 70.

2 Turn it into a git-gel as on page 78.

3 Comb it to make a Nonpareil as on page 86.

4 After creating the Nonpareil pattern, move your comb slightly to the left or right in the bath so the tines are sitting in between the previous lines. Then pull the comb back through the size, parallel to the previous lines. This makes a chevron pattern

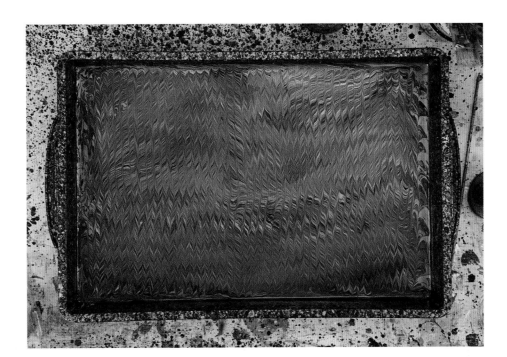

ABOVE Chevron pattern on the marbling bath.

LEFT The process of making a Chevron pattern.

Cockerell Wave

This pattern was developed by Cockerell & Sons, a highly respected British marbling and binding company that sadly closed in 2012.

Start by making a Chevron pattern as described on page 107 (shown in steps 1–3 of the papers, opposite). Then take a wide-spaced dowel comb, insert it perpendicular to the lines of the chevron, and draw it through the bath in a gentle wavy motion (see step 4, opposite). Alternatively, you can use a skewer to draw each wavy line individually, but try to make them all parallel.

ABOVE Pulling a comb with dowel teeth across a Chevron pattern to complete the Cockerell Wave pattern.

RIGHT The process of making a Cockerell Wave. It is most effective if you drop the paint in regular lines to start with.

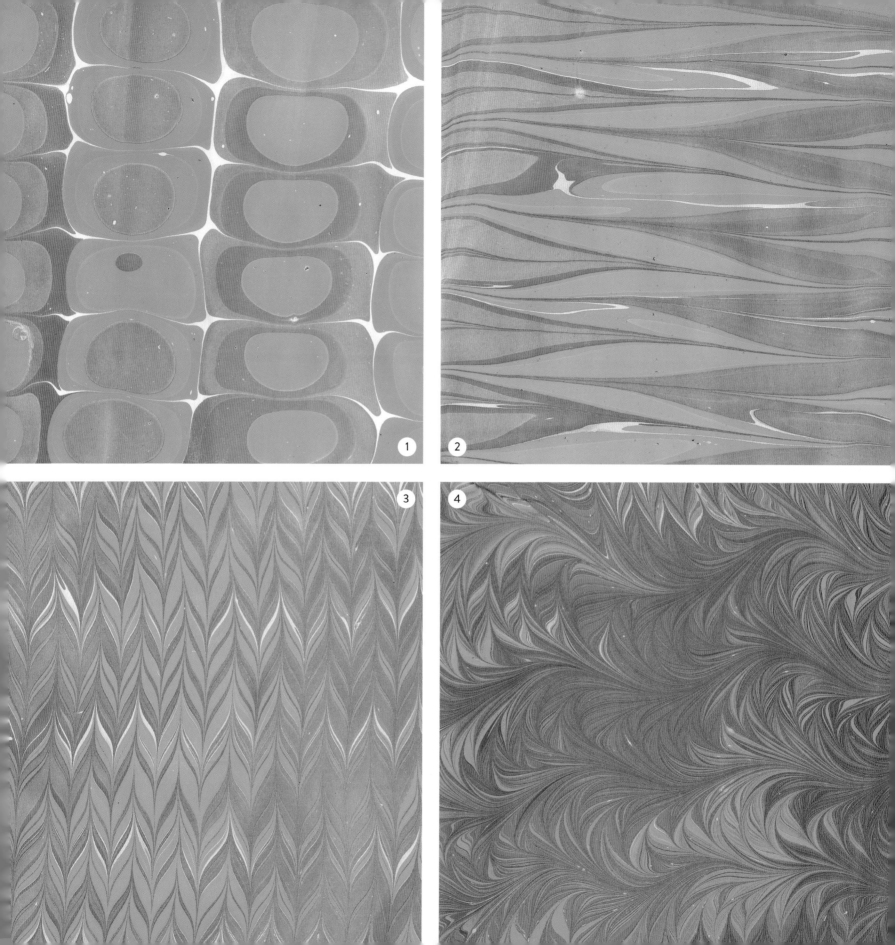

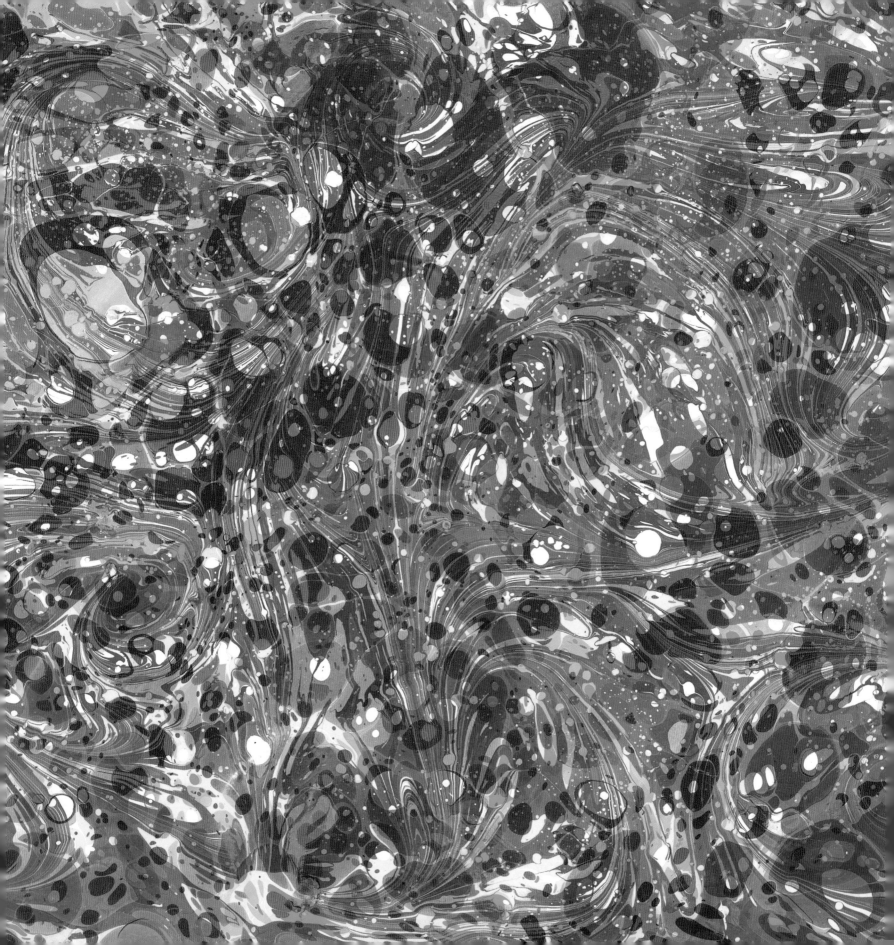

Double marbling

Marbled papers, once dried and flattened, can be mordanted and marbled straight onto again. This can create some fascinating effects as the colours and pattern layers interact. It's also a great way to revive papers that didn't quite go according to plan!

Using dark colours on top of brights

It's easy to end up with an overwhelming mush of colour and pattern with double marbling – so start by using contrasting elements in each layer. For instance, your first layer could be a celebration of bright colours, followed by a monochrome layer with sprinklings of dispersant to let the underlayer pop through in places. This produces a more muted but nuanced paper.

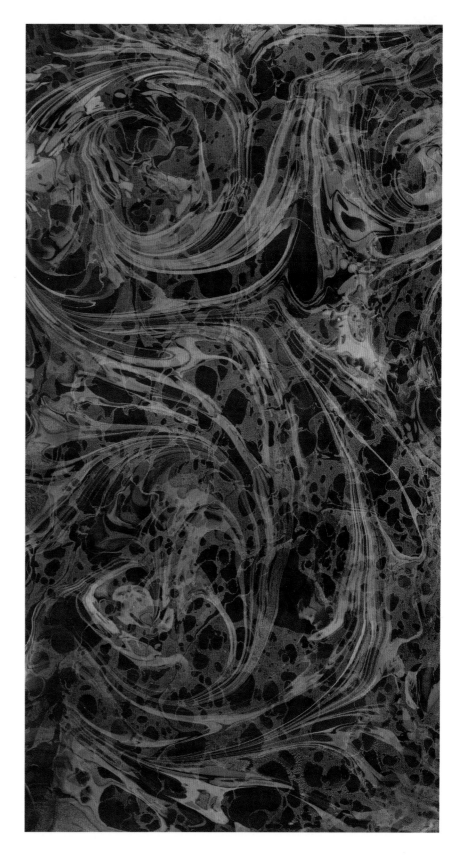

LEFT A paper marbled first in just one colour, then marbled again with bold blobs of bright primary colours.

RIGHT This paper was first marbled with white and bronze, then marbled again with an iridescent blue paint for a ghostly shine.

Blobs versus lines

Try marbling a layer of a single-colour, large Stone pattern over an initial Swirl or git-gel pattern. Choose contrasting or complementary colours for each layer to really make the finished design pop. This layering of round shapes over thin lines creates a visually exciting effect that leads the eye around the paper, with lots of interesting areas where the patterns intersect.

Layering chevrons

Once you're familiar with the Chevron technique, you might want to try out more complex designs. You can lay colours out in lines using an eyedropper, comb them into chevrons and make your first print. Then drop more lines of colour the opposite way, comb chevrons the opposite way and do another print. You can build designs in this way that look almost like woven fabric!

LEFT This paper was double marbled with bold single-colour layers, allowing the contrasting patterns to lead the eye.

RIGHT The chevron patterns that form the layers in this paper intersect in a way that is reminiscent of woven fabric.

Moving the paper to make patterns

I have covered a lot of ways to make patterns by manipulating the paint on the surface of the size – but you can also create amazing effects by controlling how the paper is laid onto it.

Spanish Wave

This is a traditional pattern, very popular in England throughout the nineteenth century. It creates a fantastic three-dimensional effect much like ripples of fabric.

To do it, grip the paper in opposite corners and slowly lay the paper down, moving it repeatedly left and right in small, fast motions. This rocking of the paper pushes the paint back and forth, causing regular undulations in opacity that make this optical illusion.

Contemporary waves

You can create interesting effects by starting to make a Spanish Wave, then lifting up the paper and rearranging your hands on the opposing corners, then laying it down and continuing the Spanish Wave technique, but laying the paper at a different angle. If you do this several times, it creates a plait-like look, especially effective with light paint on a dark-coloured paper.

Instead of laying the paper down from one corner to the other, try starting in the middle and moving it in circular motions as you lay it down. This creates exciting breaks and shifts in the pattern.

LEFT This black paper was repositioned several times as it was printed to get the interesting plait-like wave formation.

RIGHT This paper was lightly folded diagonally and then rocked onto the surface of the size from the middle outwards. The folds caused the slight peaks in the ripples.

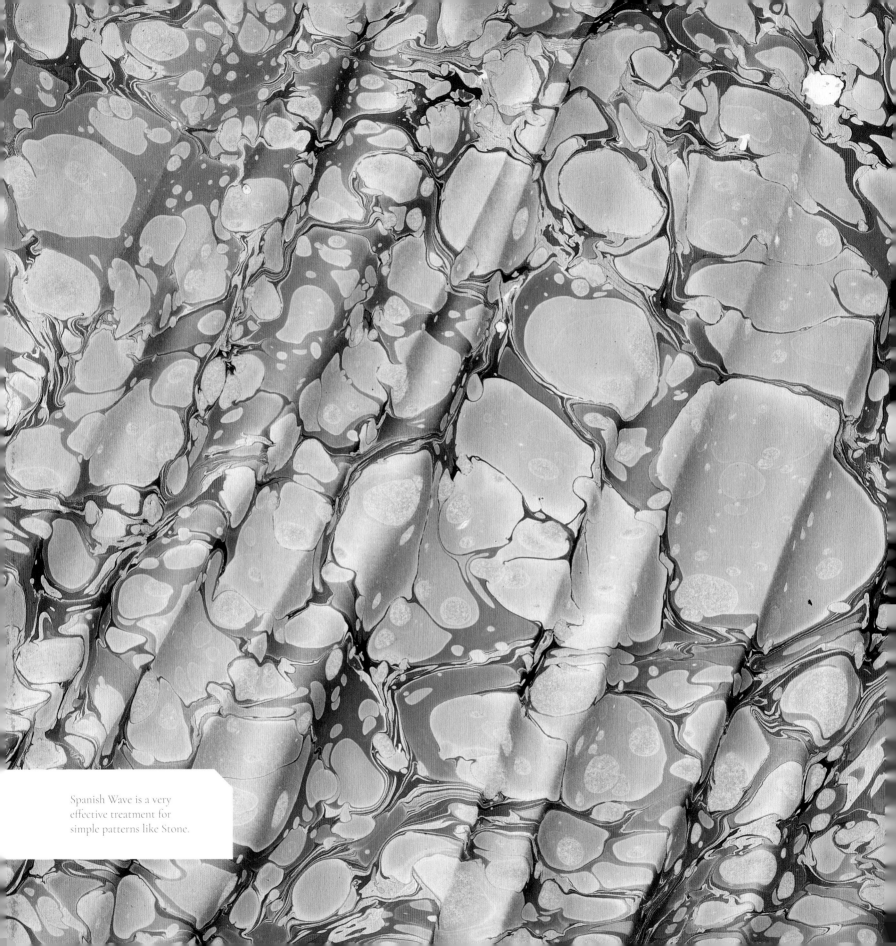

Spanish Wave is a very
effective treatment for
simple patterns like Stone.

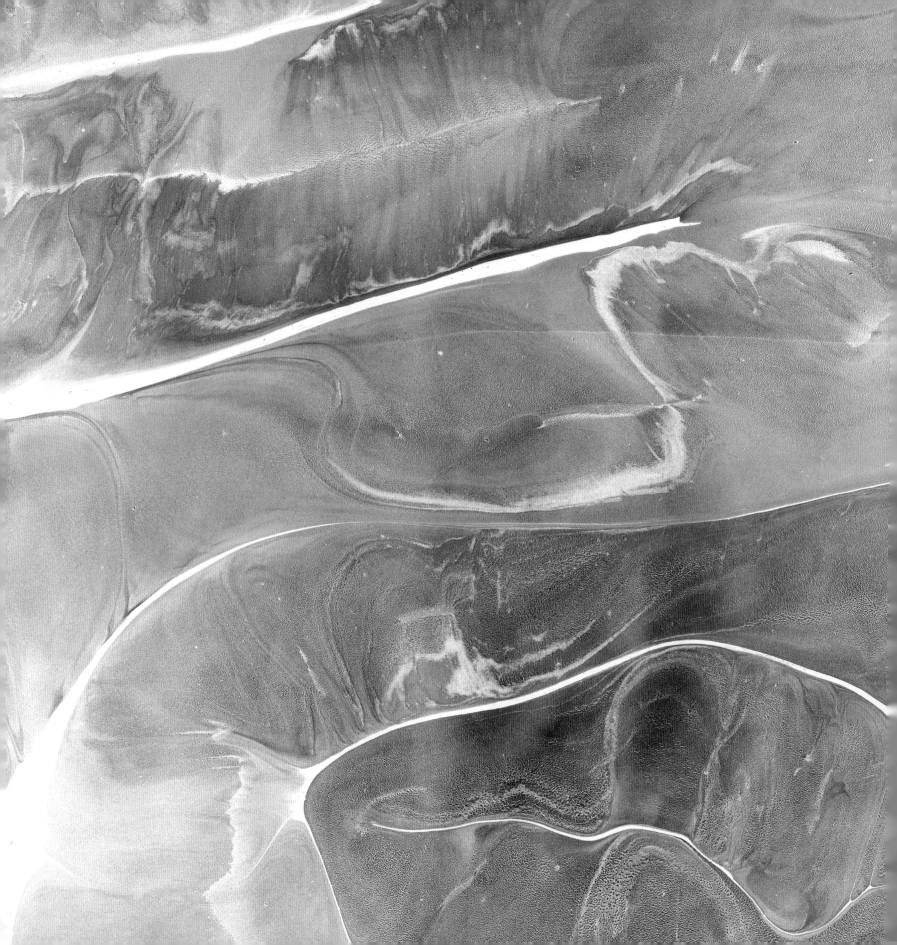

Mixing colours on the size

A traditional characteristic of marbling is the way each colour forms a flat, unblended shape separate to other colours. It can be fun to turn this on its head and play with paint that is starting to mix with another colour. The intermingling colours interact on the surface of the size for some beautiful abstract effects.

Mix up three or four different colours, putting some extra diluted dispersant into all of them. Then pour them all into the same container. Do not stir it! Take the container and slowly pour it over the size, making sure to move it as you pour so the paint isn't all distributed in the same area. There should be really interesting details where the colours are starting to combine and push against each other.

Alternatively, try sucking up a bit of each colour paint in a single pipette (don't release pressure on the bulb between each colour or it will let go of your paint!) and release over the surface of the size.

You can do this in a more controlled way by painting the tines of a rake with one colour, then dabbing a second colour over them again. When you touch the ends of the rake onto the surface of the size, the two colours should interact pleasantly. You could use this as the basis of a pattern or as a finishing effect.

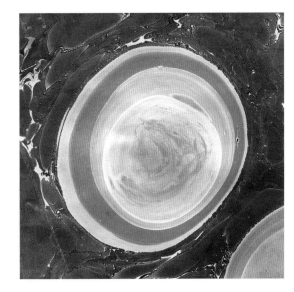

LEFT Teal and copper paint were combined in the same jar and then poured straight onto the surface of the size. This is especially effective due to the complementary colours used.

RIGHT Paint was combined within an eyedropper to create this planet-like swirling effect when dropped onto the size.

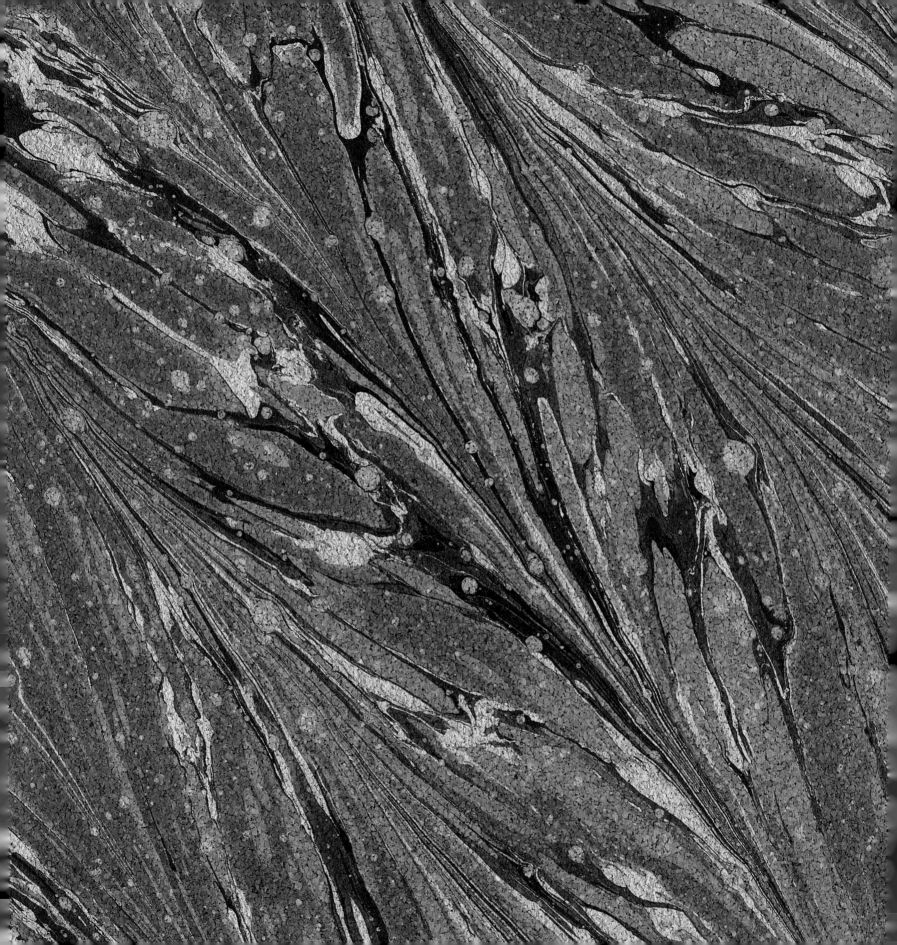

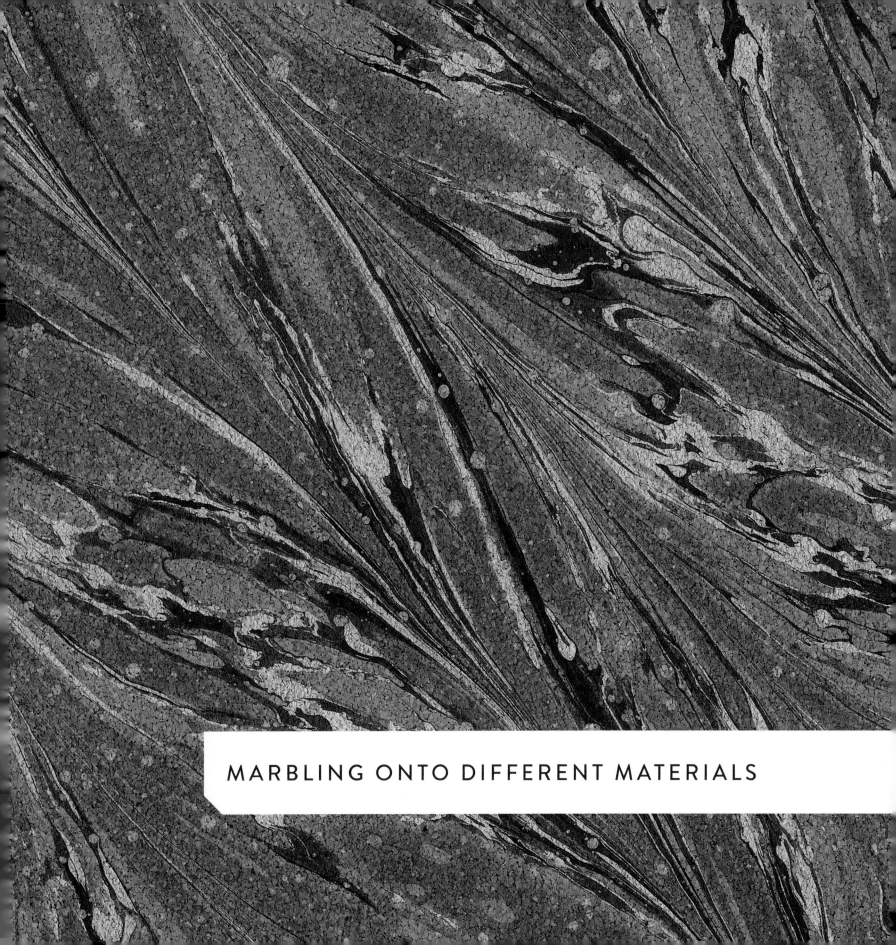

MARBLING ONTO DIFFERENT MATERIALS

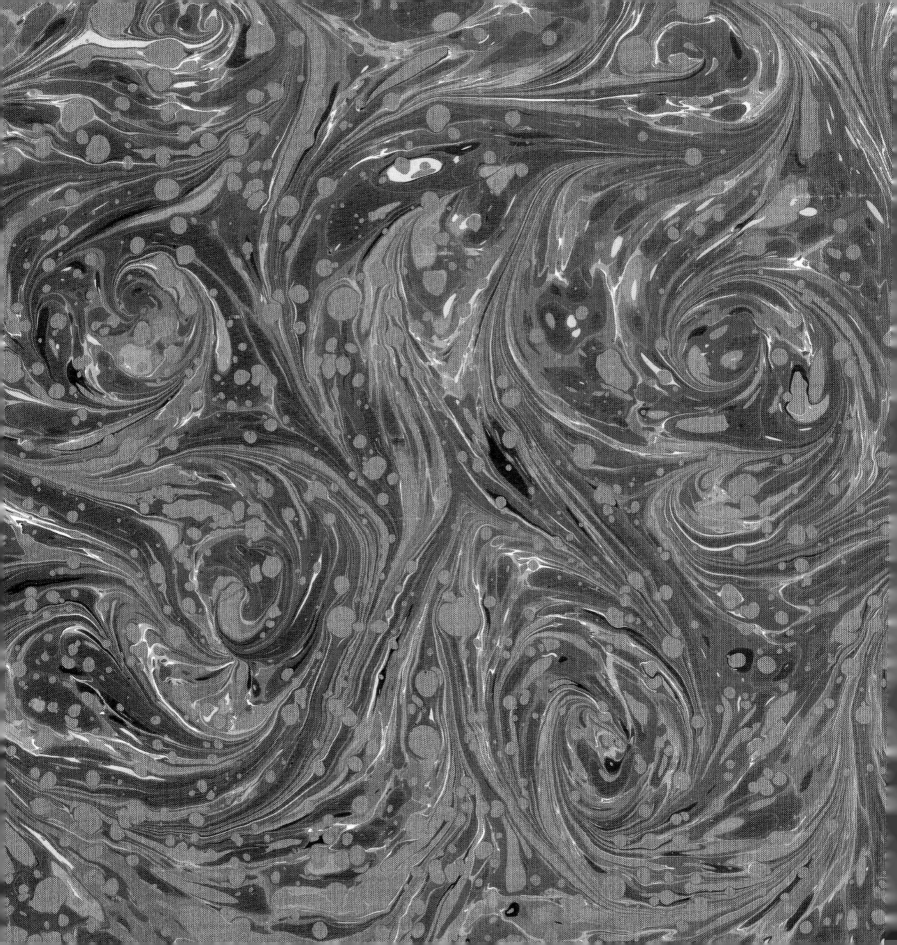

Working on alternative surfaces

Marbling is an incredibly versatile technique. It can be applied onto anything porous – if you can fit it in your marbling bath, you can marble it!

As mass manufacturing and printing increasingly offer cheaper alternatives for decorative paper, marbling is gradually moving away from its historical association with the bookbinding and publishing industry. New materials and applications for marbling are carving out new niches for the craft – it's an exciting time for marbling!

Marbling on fabric

You can marble many different types of fabric to make beautiful scarves, garments and accessories. Acrylic paint must be used when marbling onto fabric, as it's the only type of paint that will bond with the fabric to ensure it doesn't wash off.

The best types of fabric to use are smooth, natural fibres such as silk, though you can marble onto fabrics made from cotton, linen or even wool. However, the rough texture of these materials will make your colours appear dull and muted.

Your fabric will need to be mordanted – you may wish to soak it in an alum bath to ensure even coverage, but it must be allowed to dry out before marbling.

Fabric is much floppier than paper so you will need to be careful when laying it onto the marbling bath. If marbling a piece of fabric that fits entirely into your marbling bath, fix the back of it to a piece of thick paper (same size as the fabric) with masking tape. This will lend the fabric some rigidity so you can lay it onto the bath as you would paper.

If you have a larger item, such as a T-shirt or scarf, consider using an embroidery hoop to isolate an area of the item. Embroidery hoops are usually circular (but squares are available) and hold the fabric taut between an inner and outer wooden form. Gather the loose fabric up behind the hoop and carefully lower the hoop onto the surface of the bath. Be careful not to dip it into the size too far, or you could get paint on areas beyond the hoop. Remove the outer hoop, rinse, and leave to dry. This creates striking circular marbled sections.

LEFT The smoothness of this grey silk makes it ideal for marbling.

Marbled fabrics should be heat-pressed or ironed on the reverse of the fabric, between protective pressing cloths, when dry, so that the acrylic colours can bond with the material – this should prevent them from washing away.

How to marble ribbon

Use the same container you would use to marble paper – the bigger the better.
Fill a jug with water and set it beside your bath.

METHOD

1 Mordant the ribbon, either applying it with a paintbrush or dipping it in a bath of alum, and leave to dry. If painting, remember to mark the back with pencil or chalk.

2 Create a marbled pattern on the size as you would for marbling paper – for a Swirl pattern, see page 75.

3 In one hand, hold one end of the ribbon, and with the other hand, hold the ribbon further along its length. Lay the section of ribbon that's between your hands onto the size, holding the end in place so it doesn't move across the size. Don't worry about trying to fit the whole length on at once – just as much as will comfortably fit on the surface.

4 Carefully peel the ribbon from the size, making sure not to get any unmarbled areas wet.

5 Place most of the marbled ribbon into the jug of water to sit while you marble the next section. This helps to keep it out of the way too.

6 Take the next section (with a slight overlap from the marbled area – don't worry, as any double marbling will wash away) and lay it onto a fresh area of the bath in the same way.

7 Repeat until all the ribbon is marbled, give it a swish in the jug of water to ensure it is thoroughly rinsed and hang it to dry.

8 Heat press to make the ribbon colourfast.

RIGHT If you marble ribbon with a Swirl pattern, it effectively hides any areas where you might have joins in the marbling.

Marbling onto leather or cork

Leather is a very versatile material that can be used to produce a range of items from shoes to handbags or jewellery. Look out for leather that hasn't been 'finished' or treated to make it shiny and waterproof as this won't take mordant or paint very well. The lighter the colour, the brighter the marbled colours will be.

Leather can be expensive and is also problematic for people who would like to avoid using animal products – but don't worry, there is an increasing selection of materials designed to avoid these issues. My favourite is cork – naturally waterproof, sustainable and pleasant to touch, it can be used as a leather replacement, or as a material in its own right. Cork is a fascinating spongy wood made from the bark of cork oak trees, best known for its use as stoppers for wine bottles or on message boards. There have been some exciting innovations that have seen the introduction of cork 'fabric' which is super thin and flexible.

Cork and leather are fairly stiff so can be treated exactly the same as you would paper, except there's no need to flatten them once mordanted – just lay them out to dry.

LEFT Notebook with
marbled cork cover.

Marbling on wood

Wood is a fantastic material for marbling – it comes in many different types, each with its own colour and grain pattern that adds character to the finished piece. It has a multitude of uses and directly marbling it can be a great alternative to glueing on marbled papers, especially for awkward-shaped objects!

Use wood veneer for furniture, marquetry, wood-working or even to cover books as shown opposite. Solid wood or MDF shapes are a great option for sturdy decorative letters and objects.

Wood should be treated similarly to paper – mordanting should always be done on composite woods such as MDF that have a higher degree of processing, though it is not always necessary for very absorbent solid woods. It is usually better to be safe than sorry, though.

Bear in mind that the natural colour of the wood will affect your final results – more translucent paints will take on this shade, and colder colours may be made to appear warmer. Be sure to test your colours with a small piece before you do your final marbling.

Wood veneer can be tricky to keep flat – it has a natural curve to it. This can cause air bubbles when you marble it, so try flexing the veneer so it goes into the bath from the middle outwards.

BELOW A sheet of marbled wood veneer.

RIGHT A book made using a piece of marbled wood veneer mounted onto the cover – this adds extra durability to the book.

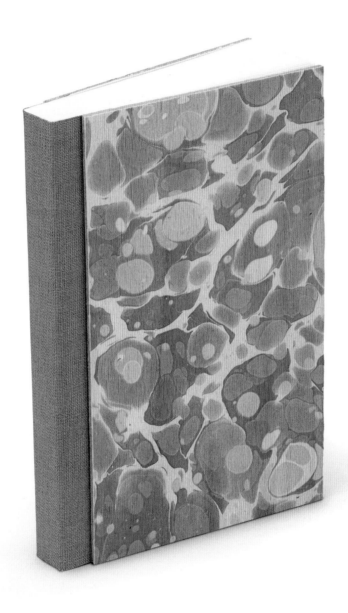

Marbling three-dimensional objects

The process for marbling objects is a little different from how paper marbling is done – rather than creating a pattern on the surface and then simply picking that up, the pattern is created as the object is dunked into the size. The paint going up the sides of the object creates the pattern – so you never know exactly how the piece will come out!

Ceramics

Ceramics are an absolute joy to marble – their smooth, white surface doesn't interfere with the tone of your colours and is ideal for bold colours and metallic paints, which come out beautifully.

You will need to use bisque fired ceramics – this means they have been fired once and no longer have any moisture within them. They are still very absorbent though, which means that there is usually no need to mordant them before marbling – the colours adhere upon contact. It also means they become touch-dry extremely quickly, useful for practical space-saving purposes!

You may be familiar with paint-you-own pottery cafés – these use bisque ceramics and can be a great source of lots of different shapes and forms of pottery.

Do bear in mind that ceramics marbled with acrylic, watercolour or gouache paint will not survive a further firing – if you want to protect your marbled ceramic, it is best to use a gloss varnish or spray sealer. Unfortunately, marbled ceramics are not food safe and anything you make should be purely decorative.

LEFT MDF letters that have been dipped into the marbling bath.

BELOW Dipping items such as these concrete planters three quarters of the way into the marbling bath and then removing them can leave an attractive edge that shows off the qualities of the material you are using.

How to marble ceramic baubles

Use a deep container or bucket to contain your size. Remember to leave enough space between the size and the top of the container for the bauble to displace it as it is dunked. You may want to wear gloves to protect your fingers as they usually end up in the size too!

METHOD

1 Make your preferred marbled pattern using your desired colours.

2 Try to hold your bauble in a place that won't be seen – baubles often come with a metal cap, which provides a handy spot for gripping.

3 Slowly and smoothly dip the bauble into the size. You will find that the hollow bauble will need a bit of force to be pushed beneath the surface – try to keep an even pressure from the top or it will slip to the side.

4 Try slowly rotating the bauble as you dunk it to produce an attractive swirling pattern.

5 Remove the bauble from the size. Ceramic is very absorbent so you run the risk of inadvertently double-marbling your bauble as it comes back out of the size. Rinsing immediately should remove any excess paint, or you can try removing the leftover paint on the size with some newspaper while the bauble is submerged (this can be tricky – you may need an extra pair of hands!).

6 Thread string through the bauble's loop and hang up to dry for about 15 minutes.

LEFT Marbled ceramic baubles make for very effective planet-like decorations.

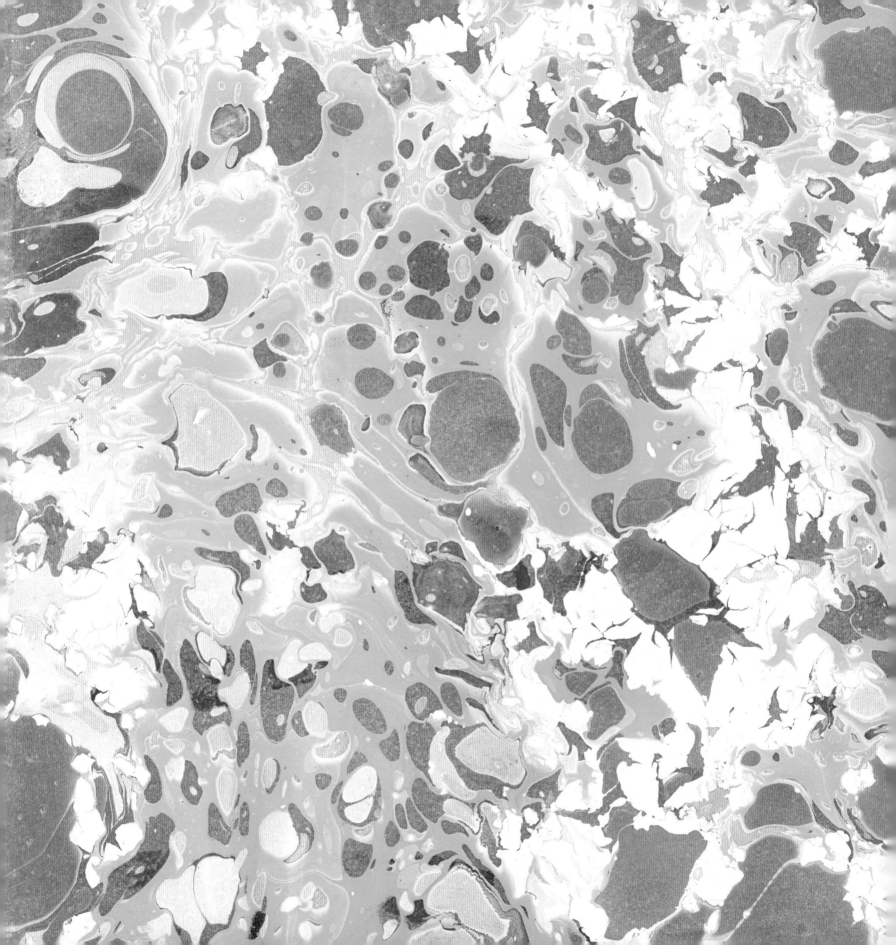

TROUBLESHOOTING

Pale line or several lines running across the paper

This is called a hesitation line (see 1, right), and it occurs when there is a pause when the paper is being lowered onto the size. Make sure that you are using supple paper (it can help to mist it with alum solution to keep it flexible if you're doing a long run and your paper is stiff) and aim to place it on the surface in one smooth, fluid motion. Practice makes perfect with this!

Round holes in the pattern

These are most likely air bubbles that occur where air gets caught between the paper and size as you lower it onto the surface (see 2, below). This can happen when mordanted paper warps as it dries, making the surface uneven. Make sure to flatten your papers directly after you mordant them.

Don't drop your paper when you're laying it onto the size, either, as this can trap air under the paper – hold both corners until they are fully laid onto the size. It can help to mist your papers with alum solution to keep them damp and flexible.

Acrylic colours are coming out really pale – how can I make them brighter?

Often the simple reason is that you may not be putting enough paint on your marbling bath. The more you put on, the more the patches of previously applied colour are displaced and pushed together, making them more saturated and bright.

Some brands of acrylic paint have a high amount of chemical dispersant mixed in during manufacturing, and this makes them expand like crazy on the marbling bath. You may find that certain paints just don't want to be pushed back by subsequent colours, or even cause subsequent colours to sink. You can try 'boosting' the other colours with a dispersant but it might be simpler to try out a different paint brand or colour.

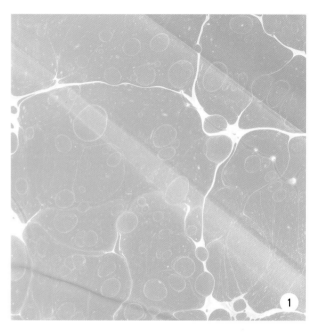

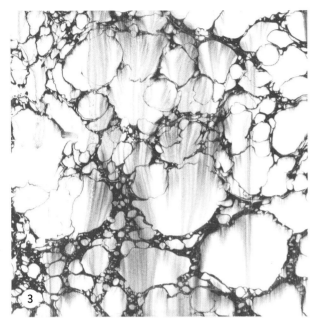

Paint is washing off the paper

Are you mordanting your paper before you start marbling? You must prepare your paper by covering it with a solution of alum (see page 30) and water, otherwise some paints won't 'stick' to the surface of the paper and wash off heartbreakingly as you rinse your paper (see 3, left).

If you are mordanting your paper, make sure you have marked the back of the paper so you're not marbling on the wrong side (sounds obvious but easily done!)

Make sure you are using paper that has not been coated with anything in the manufacturing process. The shinier the paper, the worse it takes the paint.

Paint is washing off in uneven patches

Check that you are applying enough mordant, and that you are applying it evenly enough. Try putting more alum solution on, or using a higher alum concentration.

Sometimes, when you have put too much paint on the bath, it refuses to 'take' to the paper and sits in globs on the surface (see 4, left). When you rinse the paper, these globs wash away. Try using less paint or thinning it with a dispersant.

Preparation problems

Carrageenan size is super-thick and sticks to the paper

It is possible you are using the wrong grade of carrageenan. Make sure you use lambda grade for paper marbling, as kappa and iota carrageenan are used to form gels (see page 20 for more information.

If you do have the right kind of carrageenan, try lowering the ratio of carrageenan to water. It should be roughly the texture of wallpaper paste.

The carrageenan size loses its viscosity and doesn't hold patterns well

This can happen when your size is too warm. If you're marbling on a particularly hot day, make sure to open your windows to get some cool airflow in. It can also help to keep your size in the fridge prior to marbling if it's very hot.

If your size is too old, it can also cause problems. Try making a fresh batch.

Weird 'shards' and shapes are forming in paint layer and the paint won't spread out evenly

This is often a problem with the water used. Particularly hard-water areas such as London and the Southeast tend to have high levels of minerals such as calcium in the water that interfere with the behaviour of the size (see right). You can use a tablespoon of water softener (such as borax alternatives) when you mix your size to try to combat this. Alternatively, consider using water filters or distilled water.

This can also be caused by alum contamination. If you are using fabric or paper that has been coated very thickly with alum, it may deposit some on the surface of the size, causing issues with the surface tension.

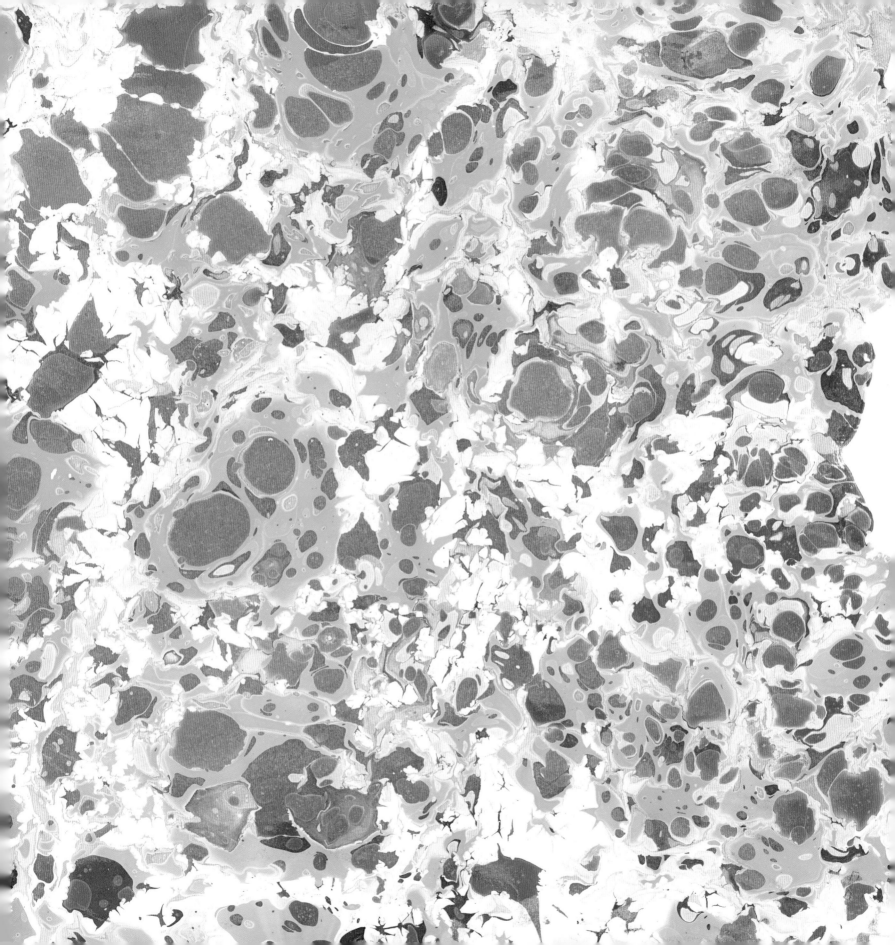

Obtaining materials

Nearly all of the tools and ingredients you need for marbling can be found at home but to help you if you're missing a few or you are unsure where to start, I've compiled a list of my favourite resources.

Aluminium potassium sulphate (alum) is easy to purchase online due to its multiple household/industrial uses - I get granules or fine crystals from eBay for a very reasonable price. You could also contact a specialist craft supply company such as George Weil.

Carrageenan is probably the hardest of all the marbling ingredients to find, especially the right carrageenan. You can sometimes find it on websites like eBay, but be careful to get lambda, as the other grades are more commonly available due to their use in patisseries and for brewing. Look for specialist culinary suppliers such as Chemicalloids Ltd – however these often require a minimum order of a 24kg (53lb) sack! I do offer smaller quantities through Marmor Paperie's website if you are struggling with this.

Carrageen: If you're feeling adventurous and want to try making size the traditional way, you can always go beach-combing on the West coast of Britain or Ireland and pick some of your own carrageen seaweed! For those based in the capital, it's available to buy from health-food shop Baldwins.

Ox gall is used as a dispersant in gouache and watercolours so you should be able to find ox gall in quality art supply shops. It's usually found in the 'Watercolour painting' section.

Acrylic: it's worth experimenting with all kinds of brands and colours to find the ones that work best for you. I have had good results with Liquitex (particularly their 'heavy body' range), Galeria by Windsor & Newton and Golden (but these are more expensive).

Gouache is available from most large art supply shops. I find Windsor & Newton's 'Designer' range to be very good.

Watercolour in tubes is easier than pans. There are a few different brands commonly available, though I recommend Windsor & Newton's Professional range.

Paper: This is very much a personal preference based on what you want to do with your marbled papers and the effects that you like. I have used all kinds, ranging from standard 80gsm printer paper to beautiful heavy-weight cotton fibre papers. I find that smoother papers give the most vibrant results, such as Munken's Smooth range (available in a variety of off-white shades). I recommend taking a trip to your local paper supply shop and taking a moment to get to know the different varieties, feeling the surfaces and weights for yourself. Remember to avoid papers that are described as 'sized' or have a shiny finish.

Marbling baths can be anything, as long as it is watertight and will comfortably fit a sheet of A4 (or whichever size paper you would like to marble onto) – I find stationery shops usually offer handy document boxes made of plastic with locking lids which are ideal. Professional marblers often use stainless steel trays, but these are usually made to order.

Brushes: You don't need fancy artists' brushes for marbling – anything stiff enough to hold its shape when wet will do the job. Children's paintbrushes are actually a great option as they often come in handy large packs and can be found easily in craft and toy shops. I do recommend splashing out on a few different sizes of fan brush though – these are good for evenly distributing paint.

Index

References to illustrations are in *italics*.

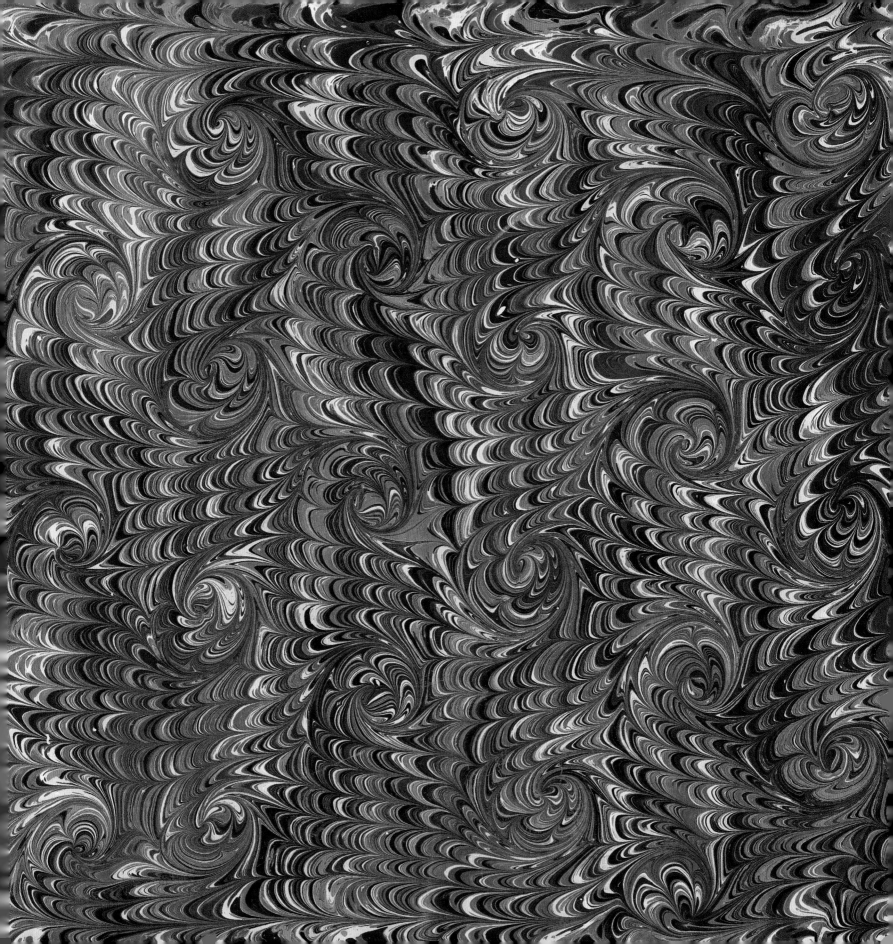

Acknowledgements

Special thanks to Margaret and Sophie McGrath, for all their time poring over versions of this book. Thanks to Jeremy Johns and Jamie Trounce for the incredible photographs. Thanks also to Andrew McGrath, Bob McGrath, Joshua Walker, Kethi Copeland and Jen Rowland for their help and support, and the Heritage Crafts Association for recognising the potential of Marmor Paperie back when I was starting out.

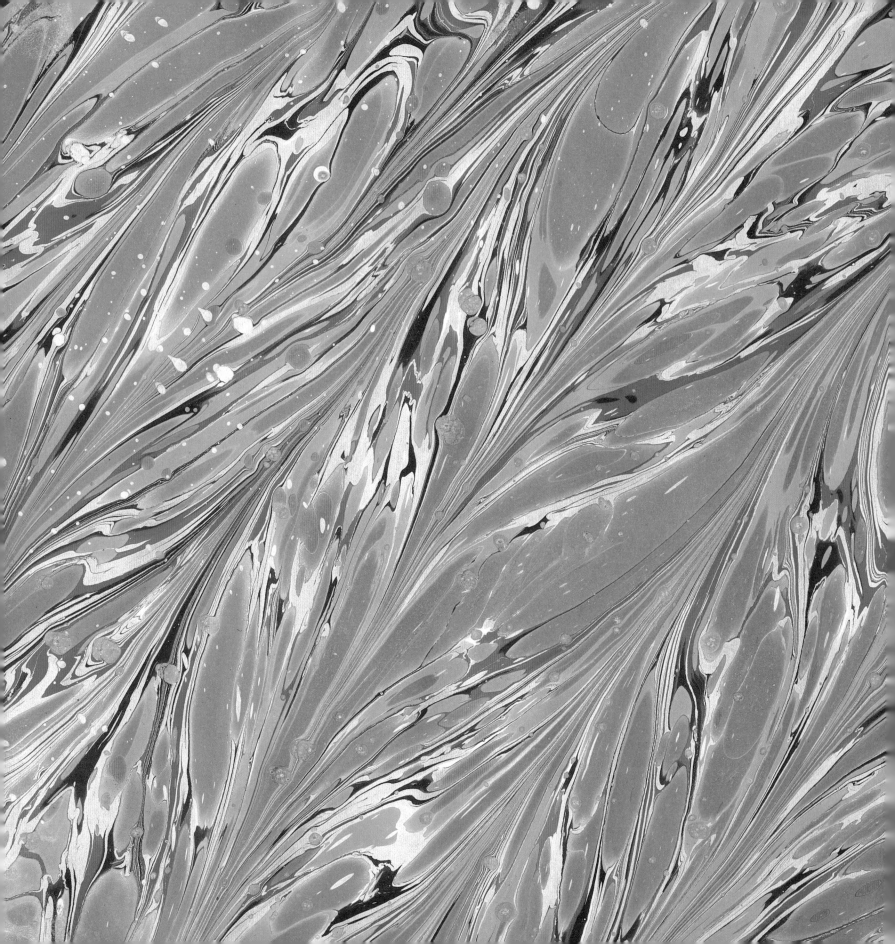